GARIBALDI

LEADERSHIP ■ STRATEGY ■ CONFLICT

RON FIELD ■ ILLUSTRATED BY PETER DENNIS

First published in 2011 by Osprey Publishing
Midland House, West Way, Botley, Oxford OX2 0PH, UK
44-02 23rd St, Suite 219, Long Island City, NY 11101, USA

E-mail: info@ospreypublishing.com

ISBN: 978 1 84908 321 8
E-book ISBN: 978 1 84908 322 5

Editorial by Ilios Publishing Ltd, Oxford, UK
Maps by Mapping Specialists Ltd
Page layouts by Myriam Bell Design, France
Typeset in 1 Stone Serif and Officina Sans
Index by Mike Parkin
Originated by United Graphics Pte
Printed in China through Worldprint Ltd

11 12 13 14 15   10 9 8 7 6 5 4 3 2 1

A CIP catalogue record for this book is available from the British Library.

www.ospreypublishing.com

Acknowledgements:

Thanks are due to Peter Harrington, Curator, Anne S. K. Brown Military
Collection, Providence, Rhode Island; Matthew Neely, Archivist,
Bodleian Library, Oxford; Cameron Robinson; Piero Crociani; and to the
staff of the Museo Storico della Fanteria, Rome, Italy.

Artist's note

Readers may care to note that the original paintings from which the
colour plates in this book were prepared are available for private sale. All
reproduction copyright whatsoever is retained by the Publishers. All
enquiries should be addressed to:

Peter Dennis, Fieldhead, The Park, Mansfield, Notts, NG18 2AT

The Publishers regret that they can enter into no correspondence upon
this matter.

Cover Image

Anne S. K. Brown Military Collection, Brown University Library.

The Woodland Trust

Osprey Publishing are supporting the Woodland Trust, the UK's leading
woodland conservation charity, by funding the dedication of trees.

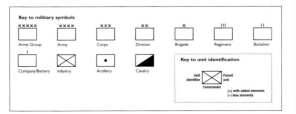

CONTENTS

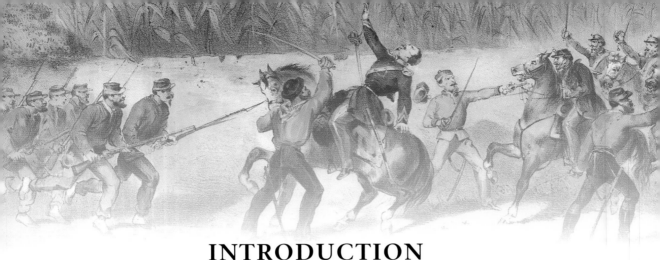

INTRODUCTION

The military genius of Giuseppe Garibaldi was defined on a high hill near Calatafimi in Sicily on 15 May 1860, when his poorly armed volunteers, known as *i Mille* ('the Thousand'), faced Neapolitan regular light infantry for the first time. Moving among his foremost troops, who were sheltered behind a terraced wall halfway up the hillside, Garibaldi waited to launch a decisive assault. As he bent low to negotiate a gap in the wall, a small piece of rock hit him on his back. Realizing that the enemy was running out of ammunition and was resorting to throwing rocks, he ordered a charge and clambered up the bank waving his sword, urging his men to follow. The *garibaldini* scrambled after him towards the crest of the hill where they were met with volley fire from the Neapolitan infantry, followed by a further hail of rock. As the two desperate bodies of men clashed, the musket butt and bayonet exacted a deadly toll, but soon the enemy fell back, rushing headlong towards Calatafimi. At that moment Garibaldi and his volunteers realized that they could take on and defeat Neapolitan regular troops. The struggle for Italian independence in 1860 had reached a turning point. By November of that year the Bourbon hold on Southern Italy had completely collapsed and within ten years the unification of the whole of Italy had been achieved.

With his black lieutenant Andrea Aguyar mounted by his side, Garibaldi is saluted by republican troops near Velletri during the defence of Rome in 1849. He wears the white mantle or cloak that often protected him from spent enemy musket balls during the height of battle. (Anne S. K. Brown Military Collection)

Garibaldi began his military career on the plains and coastal waters of Brazil and Uruguay in South America, where he first rode with rebel gauchos during the struggle for independence for the Republic of Rio Grande do Sul, and later commanded the small Uruguayan fleet against the Argentine-backed forces of Manuel Oribe. Involved in numerous actions during the latter struggle, notably at San Antonio, he gained a worldwide reputation as a formidable commander of soldiers and sailors.

With the outbreak of revolution in Europe in 1848, Garibaldi returned with his Legion to the Old World to realize his lifelong aim of liberating and uniting the people of the Italian peninsula. Despite his courage and inspired leadership during fighting against the French in the Pamphili Gardens, at Velletri and at Villa Corsini, the Republic of Rome fell in 1849 and Garibaldi escaped into the Alban hills offering only 'hunger, cold, forced marches, battles and death' to those that followed. After about five years living as a fugitive, ex-patriot and mariner he settled on the island of Caprera, north of Sardinia, where he watched and awaited events in Italy. His military reputation amongst the Austrians as '*Rötheufel*' ('red devil') was revived and further enhanced by the skill with which he commanded the

Garibaldi's European campaigns and battles, 1849–71

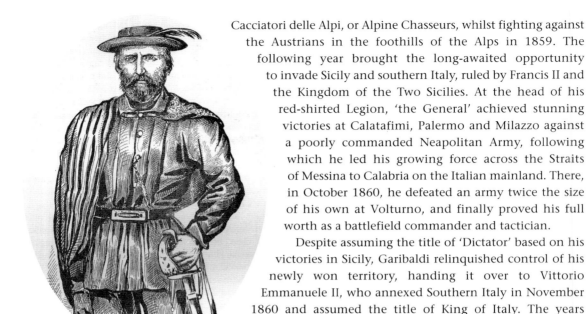

Published in 1889, this engraving depicts Garibaldi as he looked in Montevideo, Uruguay, in 1846. He wears an example of the scarlet blouse for which his Italian Legion, and later 'the Thousand', became famous. (Author's collection)

Cacciatori delle Alpi, or Alpine Chasseurs, whilst fighting against the Austrians in the foothills of the Alps in 1859. The following year brought the long-awaited opportunity to invade Sicily and southern Italy, ruled by Francis II and the Kingdom of the Two Sicilies. At the head of his red-shirted Legion, 'the General' achieved stunning victories at Calatafimi, Palermo and Milazzo against a poorly commanded Neapolitan Army, following which he led his growing force across the Straits of Messina to Calabria on the Italian mainland. There, in October 1860, he defeated an army twice the size of his own at Volturno, and finally proved his full worth as a battlefield commander and tactician.

Despite assuming the title of 'Dictator' based on his victories in Sicily, Garibaldi relinquished control of his newly won territory, handing it over to Vittorio Emmanuele II, who annexed Southern Italy in November 1860 and assumed the title of King of Italy. The years 1861–70 were filled with further, but less successful, attempts at military conquest as Garibaldi rallied support for the continued struggle, not only for the unification of Italy, but for all European nationalities. He established the International Legion with ambitions of ridding Europe of autocratic rule from 'the Alps to the Adriatic', and hoped to use his powers as a Freemason and politician to further those ends. But his efforts in battle were less successful. During further failure to capture Rome, he was shot in the foot at Aspromonte, in southern Italy, in 1863, and wounded in the leg at Mentana in 1867. Nonetheless, he achieved the only Italian victory of the Austro-Prussian War at Bezzecca in Trentino during 1866, and saw his last battlefield action when he put old animosity behind him and volunteered his services to the newly formed Third Republic, commanding the French Army of the Vosges during the Franco-Prussian War of 1870–71.

According to the eminent British historian A. J. P. Taylor, Garibaldi was 'the only wholly admirable figure in modern history'. For his battles on behalf of freedom in Latin America, Italy and France he was dubbed the 'Hero of Two Worlds'. When editing Garibaldi's *Memoirs* in 1860, Alexandre Dumas qualified this by stating: 'A man who defends his own country or attacks another's is no more than a soldier... But he, who adopts some other country as his own and makes offer of his sword and his blood, is more than a soldier. He is a hero.' The Communist revolutionary leader Karl Marx was more cynical, referring metaphorically to Garibaldi as a mercenary or 'taxi driver' who gifted the crown of Italy to Vittorio Emmanuele II via his victories in 1860. Whatever view is taken, Garibaldi understood how to inspire men on the battlefield. He proved himself to be an able tactician and, most importantly of all, was able to lead the bayonet charges at Calatafimi and Volturno that tipped the scales of battle and led to ultimate victory.

THE EARLY YEARS, 1807–47

Born in Nice, the capital of the French department of Alpes-Maritimes, on 4 July 1807, Giuseppe Garibaldi was the second of five children born to Domenico and Rosa Garibaldi. Following in the footsteps of his father, whose ship plied a trade in oil and wine along the Ligurian coast of Italy, Giuseppe was destined to go to sea and served aboard various vessels, sailing the trade routes of the world from 1824 until 1833. While moored at Taganrog, Russia, in April 1833, by which time he was a mate aboard the brig *La Clorinda*, he met Giovanni Battista Cuneo, a political immigrant from Oneglia, Italy, and member of the secret movement known as La Giovine Italia or 'Young Italy'. Founded by Genoese philosopher and politician Giuseppe Mazzini in 1831, the aim of this organization was to achieve the unification of Italy as a liberal republic. Convinced to join this society, Garibaldi dedicated the rest of his life to the struggle for the liberation of his homeland from Austrian dominance. Garibaldi finally met Mazzini at Geneva in November 1833. Joining the Carbonari ('charcoal burners') revolutionary association, he was encouraged to leave the merchant service and enlist in the Royal Piedmontese Navy in an effort to spread mutiny in its ranks. When a planned insurrection in Genoa was discovered during February 1834 he fled to Marseilles, following which he was sentenced to death *in absentia* by a Genoese court.

Finding his way to Brazil via Tunisia under the assumed name 'Joseph Pane', Garibaldi took up the cause of independence of the republic of Rio Grande do Sul, and joined the gaucho rebels known as the *farrapos* ('tatters' or 'rags'), who were fighting to free themselves from Brazilian rule. During this conflict he met Ana Ribeiro da Silva, better known as Anita. In October 1839 she joined him on his ship, the *Rio Pardo*, and a month later she fought at his side in the battles of Imbituba and Laguna. In 1841 the couple moved to Montevideo, Uruguay, where Garibaldi worked as a trader and teacher of mathematics. They married the following year, eventually producing four children – Menotti, Rosita (who died aged four), Teresa and Ricciotti.

Incapable of settling down for too long, Garibaldi took up the cause of the recently established Republic of Uruguay when it was threatened by the conservative forces of Manuel Oribe, which were backed by the Argentine dictator Juan Manuel Rosas in 1842. Forming a legion of Italian ex-patriots known as the Italian Legion, he helped defend the city of Montevideo against the forces of Oribe until 1848. His Legion adopted a flag with a black field, representing Italy in mourning, with Vesuvius at its centre symbolizing the dormant power in their homeland. Although there is no contemporary mention of the garment, it is believed that the Italian Legion first wore red shirts as part of their uniform in Uruguay, having obtained them from a mercantile house in Montevideo where they were intended for export to the slaughtering and salting establishments for cattle at Ensenada and other places in the Argentine provinces. Camouflaging the blood of men rather than animals, the red shirt was to become the symbol of Garibaldi and his

This scene from the 'Garibaldi Panorama' by Englishman John James Story depicts the aftermath of the battle that took place on the river Paraná in June 1842 between the Uruguayan flotilla commanded by Garibaldi and the naval forces of Manuel Oribe. After running out of ammunition for his guns, Garibaldi was forced to order his vessels burned while their crews escaped ashore in small boats. (Anne S. K. Brown Military Collection)

followers throughout many of their campaigns and battles in South America and Europe.

Helped by his old and experienced friend, Francesco Anzani, who was a far more capable organizer than himself, Garibaldi trained the Legion to become a skilful and dedicated fighting force. He instilled in them the belief that they were not merely fighting for the independence of Uruguay but for the future of their own country. In 1845 he occupied Colonia del Sacramento and Isla Martín García, and led the controversial sack of Gualeguaychú. Displaying the courage in the heat of battle for which he gained renown, he achieved important victories at Cerro and San Antonio. At Cerro on 17 November 1845 he bravely led the Legion in a charge in order to retrieve the body of a republican officer who had wandered into enemy lines. Similarly, at San Antonio in 1846, about 150 men of his Legion made a stand against 1,200 cavalry and 300 infantry. After hours of murderous mêlée under a scorching hot sun, during which Garibaldi had his horse shot from under him but remained personally unscathed, he led a night-time bayonet charge that shattered the enemy lines and succeeded in linking up with reinforcements. News of these brave deeds was spread by Mazzini in papers such as *L'Apostolato Repubblicano*, and the fame of the Italian Legion and its inspired commander spread throughout Europe.

Garibaldi became a Freemason during his time in South America, taking advantage of the asylum its lodges offered to political refugees of European countries governed by despotic regimes hostile to democratic or nationalistic movements. This development was to have a major influence on both his military and political career, particularly from 1860 onwards. In Montevideo during 1844 he was initiated by an irregular lodge not recognized by the main international Masonic movement. Later the same year he regularized his position by joining the Les Amis de la Patrie lodge of Montevideo under the Grand Orient de France. He subsequently attended the Masonic lodges of New York in 1850 and London in 1853–54, where he met several supporters of democratic internationalism whose anti-papal stance was influenced by socialism.

Despite fame and success in South America, the fate of his homeland continued to concern Garibaldi. The election of the liberal Pope Pius IX in 1846 caused a sensation among Italian patriots, both at home and in exile. When news of the Pope's initial reforms reached Montevideo, Garibaldi wrote the following letter, dated 12 October 1847: 'If these hands, used to fighting, would be acceptable to His Holiness, we most thankfully dedicate them to the service of him who deserves so well of the Church and of the fatherland. Joyful indeed shall we and our companions in whose name we speak be, if we may be allowed to shed our blood in defence of Pius IX's work of redemption.'

In 1847 Garibaldi offered Gaetano Bedini, the apostolic nuncio at Rio de Janeiro, the service of his Legion for the liberation of the Italian peninsula. News of the outbreak of revolution in Palermo in January 1848, and revolutionary agitation elsewhere, encouraged Garibaldi to at last lead some 60 members of his Legion home to begin the fight for the unification of Italy.

THE HOURS OF DESTINY, 1848–60

The War of 1848–49

The revolution in Italy began in September 1847 when riots inspired by liberals broke out in Reggio Calabria and Messina in the south and were put down by the troops of Ferdinand II, King of the Two Sicilies, who earned the nickname 'Re Bomba' ('King Bomb') for ordering the bombardment of Messina and Palermo at that time. On 12 January 1848 a rising in Palermo, Sicily, against the rule of Ferdinand spread throughout the island and served as a spark for revolution throughout the Italian peninsula, which spread throughout much of Western Europe. Landing at Nice, his birthplace, in April 1848, Garibaldi offered his services to the liberal Charles Albert, King of Sardinia, who was attempting to oust the Austrians from Piedmont and Lombardy in northern Italy. Faced with rejection at Genoa, Garibaldi accepted a commission under the weak provisional government of Milan in Lombardy and was sent with a small and poorly armed force to Bergamo, only to learn that disaster had befallen the main royalist army. Completely routed at Custoza on 25 July, the forces of Charles Albert retreated to Milan, where an armistice was signed with the Austrians.

Feeling betrayed but not defeated, Garibaldi determined to carry on the struggle against Austria in the Alps and waged a short campaign in the mountain villages around lakes Maggiore and Varese from 14 August 1848. Although driven across the Swiss border by 27 August, he displayed his genius for guerrilla warfare for the first time on the Italian peninsula during small actions near Morazzone, and ensured for himself the future support of revolutionaries throughout Italy.

Determined to strike further blows on behalf of Italian independence, he sailed with about 70 men for Sicily. While anchored at Leghorn in Tuscany, he was persuaded to land in hope of placing himself at the head of the Tuscan liberal forces. Rejected there, he marched overland to Bologna where he managed to recruit many more followers. Watchful of his every move, the papal authorities expected him to go next to Venice to join in its defence against the Austrians. Meanwhile, popular opinion turned against the liberal Pope Pius IX when he refused to condone war with Austria. Revolution in the Papal States was precipitated by the assassination of the conservative Minister of the Interior Pellegrino Rossi on 15 November 1848, following which the Swiss Guards were disarmed, making the Pope a prisoner in his palace. Following the escape and flight of Pius IX to Gaeta in the Kingdom of the Two Sicilies, the Roman Republic was proclaimed on 9 February 1849, under the control of a triumvirate consisting of Carlo Armellini, Giuseppe Mazzini and Aurelio Saffi. Elected to the Roman Constituent Assembly, Garibaldi took up his seat having determined that the defence of Rome was the most valuable service to be rendered to the Italian cause.

Intent on crushing the upstart Republic and returning Pius IX to his rightful place in Rome, the Catholic dynasties of Western Europe reacted quickly and marched on northern Italy. On 25 April 1849 about 10,000 French troops under General Charles Oudinot landed at Civitavecchia on the coast north-west of Rome, while Spain sent 4,000 men under General Fernando Fernández de Córdova to Gaeta, where the Pope had sought refuge. The next day the French sent a staff officer to meet with Mazzini to insist that the Pope be restored to power. The revolutionary Roman Assembly authorized Mazzini to resist the French by force of arms amid thunderous shouts of '*Guerra! Guerra!*' Republican resolve to fight was stiffened by the long-delayed triumphal entry into Rome of the charismatic Garibaldi on 27 April, who was appointed as a brigadier-general in the Republican Army. This was followed two days later by the arrival of the Lombard Bersaglieri, commanded by Colonel Luciano Manara, who had recently driven the Austrians from the streets of Milan. The wall protecting Janiculum Hill to the south-west was hastily reinforced, and the villas on the outskirts of the city were garrisoned and fortified.

The siege of Rome, 1849

On 30 April 1849, out-of-date maps used by Oudinot led him to march to the Porta Pertusa, a gate that had been walled up some time before. Based on the fact that they had experienced no resistance when they landed at Civitavecchia, the French expected to march quietly into Rome, and were without large siege guns or scaling ladders. Hence, the first shot from the Rome defences was mistaken for the noonday signal gun. Watching the French make several unsuccessful attempts to climb the Vatican walls and then withdraw a distance to regroup, Garibaldi saw his opportunity and ordered forward 300 men of the blue-coated Students' Corps. These untrained young volunteers clambered down out of the Pamphili Gardens, clashed with eight companies of the French 20th Infantry beneath the arches of the Pauline Aquaduct, and were

Totally ill-prepared for the fierce opposition they were about to receive, French troops under General Charles Oudinot advance into Rome on 30 April 1849 in this engraving by Janet-Lange published in the French journal *Illustration, Journal Universel*. (Anne S. K. Brown Military Collection)

driven back up the slope. Ordering forward elements of his Legion, which was also forced back by regular troops, Garibaldi was forced to send for help from the reserves in the city. As about 800 Bersaglieri and other republican troops arrived, he seized the moment. Although wounded in the side he remained mounted and rallied his legionaries, going on to lead a counter-attack.

For a time the outnumbered French held their ground, but after repeated attacks, during which a French officer described the defenders as being 'as wild as

dervishes, clawing at us even with their hands', they were forced back from the viaduct into the vineyards and open country beyond. They left behind them 365 prisoners and about 500 dead and wounded. However, despite Garibaldi's urging, Mazzini was loath to follow up his success, as he had not expected an attack by the French and hoped that the Roman Republic could befriend the French Republic. The French prisoners were treated as *ospiti della guerra*, or 'guests of war', and sent back to their own lines with republican tracts citing Article V of the most recent French constitution: 'France respects foreign nationalities. Her might will never be employed against the liberty of any people.'

On 4 May 1849, Garibaldi was finally permitted to leave Rome to fend off a threatened attack on the southern side of the river Tiber by the Neapolitan army of King Ferdinand II of the Two Sicilies. Five days later, while standing with his staff on the walls of the Castel San Pietro, which stood on high ground to the north of Palestrina, Garibaldi observed General Fernandino Lanza's 5,000 troops approach from Valmontone in two long, straggling columns. Not content to wait for the Neapolitans to attack, he sent his men hurtling down the slopes and through the cobbled streets of the town to throw the enemy back. Within three hours the fierce engagement was over, and Ferdinand II's troops were in full retreat. Meanwhile, threatened with further attacks on Rome by the French, Mazzini summoned Garibaldi back the next day, and on 11 May he led his exhausted troops back into the city.

With the arrival in Rome of French consul-general Ferdinand de Lesseps (later builder of the Suez Canal) on a diplomatic mission from Paris on 15 May, hopes were raised for a negotiated peace. Unbeknownst to Lesseps, he was being used by the French government to gain time to build up a military presence outside the gates of Rome. Part of the vague negotiations involved the Triumvirs agreeing that the French force should remain where it was to protect Rome from the Austrians approaching from the north and the Neapolitans who were threatening from the south. Meanwhile, Garibaldi was

Although wounded in the side during the defence of Rome, Garibaldi rallied his legionaries and led a counter-attack through the Pamphili Gardens on 30 April 1849, shouting: 'Come on, boys, put the French to flight like a mass of carrion! Onward with the bayonet, Bersaglieri!' (Anne S. K. Brown Military Collection)

The defence of Rome, 1849

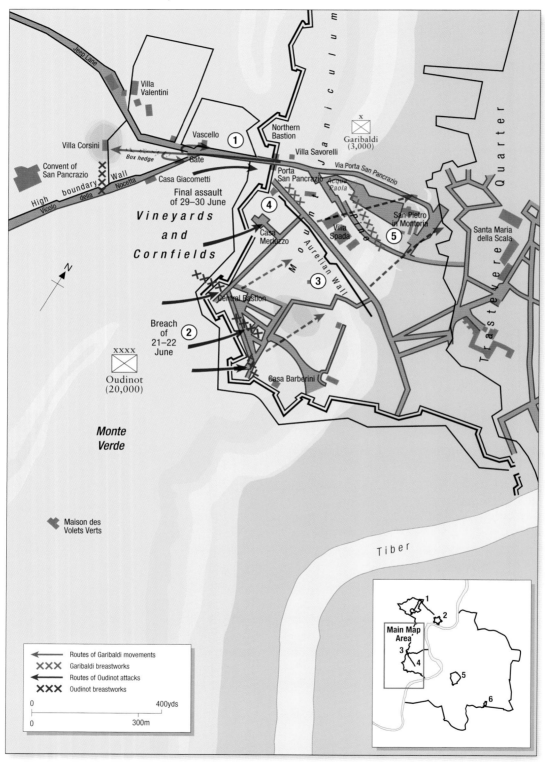

Jeep Lane

Villa Valentini

Vascello ①

Northern Bastion

Villa Savorelli

x
Garibaldi (3,000)

Villa Corsini

Box hedge

Gate

Porta San Pancrazio

Via Porta San Pancrazio

Acqua Paola

San Pietro in Montorio

Santa Maria della Scala

Convent of San Pancrazio

High   boundary   Wall   della   Nocetta

Vicolo

Casa Giacometti

Final assault of 29–30 June

Vineyards

and

Cornfields

④

Casa Merluzzo

Villa Spada

⑤

Aurelian Wall

③

Central Bastion

Breach of 21–22 June

②

xxxx
⊠
Oudinot (20,000)

Casa Barberini

Monte Verde

Maison des Volets Verts

Tiber

Routes of Garibaldi movements
XXX Garibaldi breastworks
Routes of Oudinot attacks
XXX Oudinot breastworks

0   400yds
0   300m

Main Map Area

once again permitted to leave Rome to attack the latter force. On this occasion he was subordinate to Colonel Pietro Roselli, a professional soldier and Roman, who commanded a force of 11,000 volunteers and guerrillas. Although nominally in command of the central division of Roselli's small army, Garibaldi spent much of his time in the advance guard. As he rode along the Velletri road from Valmontone during the early hours of 19 May, he discovered that the Neapolitans were retreating south from the nearby Alban Hills, having been persuaded by the French to desist from any further involvement in the campaign. Determined that they should not escape, Garibaldi ordered his advance guard to attack and sent a courier to Roselli asking him to hurry forward his own central division. After issuing insubordinate but tactically correct orders, he watched as Angelo Masina's small unit of about 40 Bolognese lancers in their colourful blue-and-red uniforms charged headlong down the road, only to come reeling back having been stopped by a much larger force of Neapolitan cavalry. Disgusted with this performance, Garibaldi, accompanied by his black aide-de-camp Aguyar, drew up his horse in the path of the retreating lancers. As they came galloping back towards him, with the banks either side of the road too steep to take avoiding action and unable to control their frightened horses, the lancers knocked their commander and his aide to the ground and trampled over them. Bruised and entangled with his saddle and stirrups, Garibaldi could not get to his feet. With the Neapolitan cavalry approaching, he would have been captured had it not been for a group of young legionaries who came to his rescue and carried him to safety.

By the time Roselli arrived with the main body of his army, the advance guard had resumed the offensive and had entered Velletri, driving the alarmed Neapolitan troops before them. But the cautious commander-in-chief was concerned that Garibaldi had committed his troops too hastily, and called a halt to the advance in order to consolidate his position. The republican force spent that night in Velletri and the bruised and disappointed Garibaldi rested in a bed previously occupied by Ferdinand II. The next morning he continued to insist that a full-scale attack would drive the demoralized Neapolitans back across the frontier from whence they came, but his advice was ignored. With news that the Austrians were advancing

Opposite:

1 Garibaldi responds to the French attack on Rome on 3 June 1849 by launching a counter-attack on a battalion of French infantry occupying Villa Corsini, about 400m outside the Porta San Pancrazio. After several hours of bloody combat, his troops are driven back into the defensive works.

2 On 21 June French assault parties storm through the breaches in the Janiculum defences following a ferocious bombardment, and capture the Central and Casa Barberini Bastions.

3 Garibaldi disobeys orders to counter-attack and withdraws his troops to an inner line of defence along the Aurelian Wall.

4 While the Romans attempt to celebrate the Feast of Saints Peter and Paul on 29 June 1849, the French breach Casa Merluzzo and capture the Porta San Pancrazio.

5 With his position behind the Aurelian Wall enfiladed, Garibaldi has no choice but to withdraw his troops. The French triumphantly enter Rome four days later, as he escapes into the Alban Hills with the remainder of his Legion.

Inset map showing outline of Rome's defences:

1 Vatican Palace
2 Castel Sant' Angelo
3 Porta San Pancrazio
4 Aurelian Wall
5 Monte Palatino
6 Lateran Palace

This engraving by Eduardo Matania depicts Garibaldi and Aguyar attempting to stop the retreat of Masina's lancers during the action at Velletri, west of Rome, on 19 May 1849. (Anne S. K. Brown Military Collection)

rapidly across the Romagna and Marche regions of Italy towards Ancona, Mazzini recalled the bulk of Roselli's army to Rome, although he permitted Garibaldi, with his Legion and the Bersaglieri, to continue an advance towards the Neapolitan kingdom. Garibaldi was also soon summoned back to Vatican City, where the threat was growing of an Austrian attack from the north. However, the Neapolitans remained completely unnerved by the ferocity of Garibaldi's tactics at Palestrina and Velletri, and would still greatly fear him when he landed in Sicily with 'the Thousand' 11 years later.

Upon returning to Rome, Garibaldi soon learned that the real threat was from the French, not the Austrians. By the beginning of June 1849 the French had amassed an army of 20,000 men outside the city walls, and General Oudinot advised Roselli that any agreement made with Lesseps was null and void, and that he would attack on 4 June. Alarmed at this turn of events, Mazzini immediately wrote to Garibaldi for advice, but the exhausted commander was resting in his lodgings in Via delle Carozze, near Piazza di Spagna, suffering from a bout of rheumatism aggravated by the bruising sustained under the hooves of his lancers' horses at Velletri and by the wound he received in the earlier action in the Pamphili Gardens during the previous month. Rather than offer advice, and disillusioned with Roselli, he replied: 'I can exist for the good of the Republic only in one of two ways – a dictator with unlimited powers or a simple soldier. Choose! Always yours, Garibaldi.' When pressed further, he merely advised that General Giuseppe Avezzana should replace Roselli as commander-in-chief.

When the French finally attacked the republican outposts to the west of Rome on 3 June, a day earlier than expected, the sulking Garibaldi arose from his bed and resumed command of his division, which defended the Porta San Pancrazio and much of the west-facing defence works. There next ensued a bloody and futile battle as he sent first his legionaries, followed by the Bersaglieri and Masina's lancers, in repeated attempts to capture Villa Corsini, which was fortified and occupied by about 200 French regular infantry. With much of the villa destroyed by republican cannon fire and its defenders crushed under falling masonry, he eventually ordered the 9th 'Unione' Regiment, supported by other troops, through the gate and up the long hill to occupy the Corsini Gardens, only to be driven back inside the city walls, leaving hundreds of dead and wounded, including lancer commander Angelo Masina, to litter the grounds of Villa Corsini. Although Garibaldi fought this action without any of the skill with which he had previously been credited, the heroism he inspired in his troops in the defence of Rome consolidated his reputation as a commander.

Although the eventual outcome of the siege of Rome was decided by nightfall on 3 June 1849, the Romans held out until the end of the month. Throughout this period the volunteers and republican troops on Mount Janiculum and in outposts at Villa Vascello and Casa Giamometti responded as best they could to the French artillery by then established on the commanding heights of the Corsini hill. General Jean-Baptiste Philibert Vaillant conducted the French siege operations with skill and precision, and pushed his trenches ever nearer to the city walls. On the night of 21 June French assault parties broke through the breaches in the Janiculum defences following a ferocious bombardment, and captured the Central and Casa Barberini bastions. Faced with the threat of being overrun, Garibaldi was ordered by Roselli to launch an immediate counter-attack, but he refused as his troops were exhausted. Instead, he established an inner line of defence along the 10m-high (33ft) walls built by the Emperor Aurelian between AD 271 and AD 275 as protection against the barbarians from the north.

Towards the end of the siege, Garibaldi continued to fall out with the republican high command. Mazzini wanted the Republic to 'die in a holocaust of suffering and self-sacrifice' which would provide an inspiration to revolutionaries throughout Europe, while Garibaldi was prepared to evacuate the city and carry on guerrilla warfare elsewhere, stating, 'Wherever we go, there Rome be'. By 27 June the rift had deepened. Refusing to continue in command, Garibaldi ordered his Legion to withdraw from their posts in the defences, much to the horror and dismay of the Triumvirs. However, he was persuaded by Manara to order their return, if only to support the republican troops they had deserted, and at dawn the next day the legionaries resumed their posts – now wearing the red shirts Garibaldi had ordered made for them earlier that month.

On 29 June 1849, as a summer storm destroyed the Romans' attempts to celebrate the Feast of Saints Peter and Paul, the French launched their final assault, rushing through the breach near Casa Merluzzo. Engaged in bitter hand-to-hand fighting throughout the night, the Romans managed to recover control of the Aurelian Wall by dawn, but with Casa Merluzzo and the Porta San Pancrazio in French hands their position became untenable. Although Colonel Manara was fatally wounded, and his faithful servant Aguyar was dead, Garibaldi remained unscathed despite leading a last desperate charge against the enemy and being involved in the mêlée for several hours.

Garibaldi's legionaries fight their way up the steps of the fortified Villa Corsini outside the Porta San Pancrazio during the defence of Rome on 3 June 1849. Despite four main attacks, his troops failed to capture the villa. (Anne S. K. Brown Military Collection)

With the life of the Republic ebbing away, Garibaldi was summoned to Rome to attend the last session of the Roman Assembly. With clothes spattered in blood and a bent sword sticking out of his scabbard, he rejected the idea of surrender or a fight to the death in the streets, and informed the Assembly that he intended to withdraw to the hills to pursue a guerrilla war. Mazzini at last endorsed this view, but urged the entire Assembly and the Republican Army, not just the volunteers, to leave the city to seek refuge in the Appenines, where they could continue a defence of the Republic. But he was outvoted by those who wished to remain at their posts until the bitter end. Resigning along with his fellow Triumvirs, Mazzini had no wish to follow Garibaldi, and returned to exile in London.

Addressing a cheering crowd in St Peter's Square shortly afterwards, Garibaldi stated:

> I am going out of Rome. Whoever is willing to follow me will be received among my people. I ask nothing of them but a heart filled with love for our country. They will have no pay, no provisions, and no rest. I offer hunger, cold, forced marches, battles and death. Whoever is not satisfied with such a life must remain behind. He who has the name of Italy not only on his lips but in his heart, let him follow me.

The evening before the French triumphantly entered Rome on 3 July 1849, he gathered a small force of about 4,000 volunteers around the Papal Archbasilica of St John Lateran and led them quietly out through the nearby Porta San Giovanni to the hills beyond. Included in this bedraggled little army were the remains of his Legion, the Bolognese lancers, the Bersaglieri and some republican cavalrymen, plus one small cannon. Having left their three children in Nice and joined Garibaldi against his wishes six days earlier, his wife Anita rode by his side disguised in a red shirt with her hair tucked up inside a wide-brimmed hat.

Villa Corsini, siege of Rome, 1849

On 3 June 1849 Garibaldi launched numerous attacks on Villa Corsini, which stood outside the Porta San Pancrazio during the siege of Rome. The first of these was made by his own Italian Legion, wearing dark-blue coats and Calabrian hats, followed in turn by Manara's Lombard Bersaglieri with their dark-green feather plumes and 'round hats' and Masina's lancers in their dark-blue hussar jackets and red pantaloons. Reinforced towards the end of the day by the 'Unione' Regiment (the old 9th Regiment of the Papal Army) in their dress caps, frock coats and red pants, Garibaldi rallied all remaining troops and led one last desperate, but unsuccessful, assault on the shapeless ruins of the villa, which by this time was occupied by about 200 French regular infantry. With the republican forces driven back without success as darkness closed in, 'the white mantle', or cloak, worn by Garibaldi could, according to George MacCaulay Trevelyan, 'still be seen moving like a great moth on the roadway, amid the last flashes of the dying battle'.

Escape and exile

Initially marching south-east towards the Alban Hills, Garibaldi and his followers soon turned north in order to throw the French army off their trail. Also to be avoided at all costs were the Neapolitans to the south, the Austrians to the north and east and the Spanish to the west. Garibaldi hoped to reach Venice and join forces with revolutionary Daniele Manin, who was still holding out against the Austrians. Although hopeful that thousands of patriotic Italians in Umbria, Tuscany and the Romagna would rally round him along the way, he found that most of his fellow countrymen were disillusioned with the revolution and frightened of retaliation if they supported him in any way. Hundreds left the ranks of his small guerrilla army during the first night of his march. However, during his long and gruelling journey north he consolidated his reputation as one of the greatest of guerrilla leaders. By marching and counter-marching, and successfully negotiating routes considered impassable, he evaded the Austrians for four weeks. Having only worthless paper money of the Roman Republic, but using the powers bestowed on him before the dissolution of the Assembly, he fed his ever-diminishing followers by demanding loans from the towns, villages and convents on his way, which were reluctantly but peacefully granted. Any volunteers under his command who committed an act of theft or violence were summarily ordered shot by Garibaldi, as Bavarian-born Chief of Staff Gustav von Hoffstetter recalled, 'without taking the cigar out of his mouth'. Reaching Terni by 8 July 1849, the Garibaldians were joined by the remnants of a republican regiment commanded by Englishman and ex-Guards officer Colonel Hugh Forbes, which had also managed to remain under arms following the fall of Rome. A silk merchant living in Sienna and a staunch supporter of Italian independence, Forbes would later live in the United States and aid abolitionist John Brown in his plot to overthrow slavery.

Elements of the French Army at last began to close in on Garibaldi's steadily shrinking force as they reached Orvieto. Finding their route north over the mountains blocked, the exhausted revolutionaries headed west in blinding rain to Salci and the Tuscan border. Once in Tuscany, they left the French behind, as they had the Neapolitans and Spanish, but now had the Austrians to contend with. The Tuscans were also disinclined to support their cause, and closed the town gates in their face at Arezzo as they continued on a north-westerly route. With the Austrians now closing in, the Garibaldians escaped up a winding mountain path through the Scopettone Pass and struggled down into the valley of the Upper Tiber, heading towards the Adriatic coast and Venice.

With his force reduced to less than 1,500 men and even some officers deserting, Garibaldi determined to change course and seek refuge in the little republic of San Marino. As he arrived at the gates of the town of San Marino, perched on its high grey rock, to ask if Captain Regent Domenico Maria Belzoppi would take him in, the Austrians fell on his rearguard. At first too exhausted to offer any real resistance, the Garibaldians beat a disorderly retreat, only to be met by Anita Garibaldi running towards them looking for her husband. Influenced by the sight of their commander's wife in their midst, plus the steadying presence of Colonel Forbes and the sight of Garibaldi galloping out of the town to join them, they rallied and held back the Austrians.

As a result, Garibaldi was able to lead his bedraggled force into the safety of the Capuchin convent, which the friars had offered as accommodation. There he wrote his last order of the day, stating: 'Soldiers, I release you from your duty to follow me, and leave you free to return to your homes. But remember that although the Roman war for the independence of Italy has ended, Italy remains in shameful slavery.' Distrusting any negotiations with the Austrians, and having determined the location of their troops encircling San Marino, he decided to continue his attempt to reach Venice. Announcing, 'Whoever wishes to follow me, I offer him fresh battles, suffering and exile. But treaties with the foreigner, never,' he rode off, not waiting to see who followed. Although seriously ill, his wife galloped after him, and the couple were quickly joined by Ugo Bassi, chaplain of his now-defunct Legion, plus the redoubtable Colonel Forbes with staff and about 230 men. Guided silently through the Austrian lines as far as the Romagna plain by a San Marino workman, they headed for Cesenatico, a fishing village about 32km (20 miles) north of Rimini, where they commandeered several fishing smacks and forced their crews to set sail, escaping to sea.

The Austrians quickly resumed the chase at sea in longboats and pinnaces, overhauling and capturing all but three of the smacks. Among those taken was Forbes, who was subsequently imprisoned at Pola on the opposite side of the Adriatic coast in what is now Croatia. Meanwhile, the vessel carrying Garibaldi and Anita reached the lagoon waters of Comacchio, north of Magnavacca. Struggling through the breakers to the island of Bosco Eliseo, Garibaldi carried his wife ashore accompanied by Major Giambattista Culiolo, who had been wounded in the leg at Rome and limped by his side. Observing the Austrian vessels still in pursuit, local liberal landowner Gioacchino Bonnet risked his life by guiding the fugitives first to a hut in the marshes and eventually to his Zanetto farmhouse, where Anita was able to rest. With the Austrians closing in, Garibaldi refused to leave his wife behind and arranged for them both to be rowed across the lagoon. Unfortunately, the boatmen soon recognized him and, fearful of reprisals, landed and abandoned their dangerous cargo ashore near a hut where they spent the night shivering in the cold. Rescued again the next morning by two fishermen sent by Bonnet who had heard of their plight, it was another 12 hours before the relative safety of another farmhouse was reached, but Anita died while being carried to a bed. Although shattered by the loss, Garibaldi was persuaded to get away while there was still time. After instructing 'the good people to bury the body', he and Major Culiolo were led inland to Sant' Alberto, where they were given refuge in a cobbler's cottage.

Assisted in their escape by local 'patriots', Garibaldi and his companion were moved south towards Ravenna. They were seated in a small inn at Santa Lucia when a small group of Austrian soldiers entered and bought drinks.

This scene from the 'Garibaldi Panorama' depicts Garibaldi accompanied by Major Culiolo assisting the ailing Anita as they escape from Austrian troops in 1849. (Anne S. K. Brown Military Collection)

Garibaldi was not recognized as he had wisely shaved off his beard. Listening to their conversation, he learned that a strong Austrian force was approaching from the south. Hence, their guides took them over the mountains to Cerbaia where they were informed that all roads to Piedmont were heavily guarded. This forced them to cross more mountains, by now dressed as sportsmen with shotguns and dogs, in order to reach the west coast opposite the island of Elba, where a boat near the coastguard station of Portiglione carried them north to the safety of Genoa. As their boat left the shore, Garibaldi saluted the four 'patriots' who had guided him on the last leg of his escape route, calling out '*Viva l'Italia*'.

Following his landing at Chiavari, Garibaldi became an acute source of embarrassment to the Piedmontese government at Genoa, which was still struggling to overcome the consequences of its defeat by the Austrians at Novara in 1849. Only with the support of France had it retained the constitution granted by King Charles Albert, but with French support for the papacy it had been forced to abandon for the moment the liberal parties in the rest of Italy. As a result Garibaldi was arrested, but he was released following a public outcry that included an impassioned speech from one deputy who declared: 'Imitate his greatness if you can: if you are unable to do so, respect it. Keep this glory of ours in the country; we have none too much.'

In the face of such passionate protest, the government was compelled to release Garibaldi, although he was asked to leave Piedmont with the promise of a pension. Agreeing to the former, he would accept only a small pension he wished granted to his 79-year-old mother. On 11 September 1849 he left Piedmont for Tunis by way of Nice, where he was allowed to stay long enough to visit his mother, who had been caring for his three children: nine-year-old Menotti, four-year-old Teresa and two-year-old Ricciotti. Arriving at Tunis aboard the *Tripoli*, he was refused entry and brought back to the island of La Maddalena off the northern coast of Sardinia, where he remained for three weeks, following which he visited Gibraltar before finally finding refuge in Morocco.

After a nine-month stay in Tangier, where he was sometimes joined by Major Culiolo, Garibaldi sailed for New York aboard the English packet *Waterloo* on 12 June 1850, arriving at Staten Island seven weeks later in ill health and still grieving for his wife. Ignoring press reports lauding his fame, he worked with Italian ex-patriot and inventor Antonio Meucci in his candle factory on Staten Island, and enjoyed hunting, fishing and sailing with his friend until he was able to resume his occupation as a sea captain. (The Meucci/Garibaldi Museum on Staten Island is listed today on the US National Register of Historic Places and is preserved as a Garibaldi memorial.) During the longest voyage he took, which lasted two years from April 1851, he visited Andean ex-revolutionary heroine Manuela Sáenz in Peru. He left New York for the last time in November 1853 and on 21 March 1854 sailed into the mouth of the river Tyne and docked at South Shields in north-east England, as master of the sailing vessel *Commonwealth*. Welcomed enthusiastically once again by the local working class, he refused an invitation to dine with dignitaries in nearby Newcastle-on-Tyne. As a memento of his stay, an inscribed sword paid for through public subscriptions was presented to him. (His grandson and namesake, Giuseppe Garibaldi II, carried the sword to South Africa with him almost half a century later when he volunteered to fight for the British Army in the Boer War.) Garibaldi stayed in England for over a month, during which time he visited London and met Emma Roberts, an English widow, with whom he developed a passionate relationship.

Departing with a cargo of coal bound for Genoa at the end of April 1854, and accompanied by his newly found female companion, Garibaldi was granted permission by the Piedmontese government to rejoin his family at Nice, although his mother had died two years earlier. In need of a place to settle with his children, he used a legacy from the death of his brother to buy the northern half of the Italian island of Caprera, north of Sardinia, where he built a house and devoted himself to agriculture. He also had an affair with Baroness Maria Espérance von Schwartz, a rich and romantic novelist and travel writer, who had sailed to La Maddalena, opposite Caprera, in the hope of obtaining permission to translate Garibaldi's memoirs into German.

The Second Italian War of Independence, 1859

During the years following 1849, Conte Camillo di Cavour, Prime Minister of the Kingdom of Piedmont-Sardinia, had realized he could not defeat Austria alone and had sought allies, partially through the participation of Piedmont in the Crimean War. In the peace conference at Paris that followed that conflict he attempted to bring attention to efforts for Italian unification. He found Britain and France sympathetic to his cause but entirely unwilling to go against Austrian wishes, as any movement towards Italian independence would necessarily threaten Austria's territory in Lombardy and Venetia. However, private talks between Napoleon III and

Cavour at Plombières after the conference identified the French Emperor as the most likely candidate for aiding Italy, though he was still not committed to the cause.

On 14 January 1858 Italian revolutionary Felice Orsini led an attempt to assassinate Napoleon III, which brought widespread sympathy for the cause of Italian unification and had a profound effect on Napoleon himself, who was now determined to help Piedmont against Austria in order to end the revolutionary activities that the governments inside Italy might otherwise allow to develop. As a result he signed a secret alliance with Piedmont against Austria, which stipulated that France would help her fight against Austria if attacked. In return, Piedmont would give Nice and Savoy to France, while Piedmont would annex Tuscany and Emilia. This arrangement served both countries, as it helped the Piedmontese plan for unification of the Italian peninsula under King Vittorio Emmanuele II, of the House of Savoy, and weakened Austria, a major opponent of the French Empire. Unable to get French help unless the Austrians attacked first, Cavour provoked Vienna with a series of military manoeuvres close to the border. On 23 April 1859 Austria issued an ultimatum demanding the complete demobilization of the Piedmontese Army. When this was refused, Austria declared war on Piedmont six days later, thus drawing the French into the conflict.

Wishing to meet him as 'a matter of great importance', Cavour had already invited Garibaldi back to Piedmont at the beginning of March 1859, where he was informed of most of what had been agreed with Napoleon III, although no mention was made about the fate of his birthplace Nice, or of Savoy. Back in Genoa, Garibaldi announced enthusiastically, 'This time we shall do it!' However, fellow republicans such as Agostino Bertani were less convinced and shared the view of Mazzini, who condemned the war, claiming it would lead to a Kingdom of Northern Italy, which had been a French dependency under Napoleon. Undeterred, Garibaldi began the enlistment of volunteers, and on 17 March he was commissioned as a major-general of the Royal Army of Piedmont and ordered to form the Cacciatori delle Alpi, or Alpine Chasseurs.

With the Cacciatori delle Alpi

Made up for the most part of those volunteers not holding Piedmontese citizenship, the Cacciatori were formed into three regiments, each containing two battalions of 500 men. The first regiment was organized under Enrico Cosenz, who had fought for Manin's republic in Venice in 1849; the second was commanded by Giacomo Medici; and the third was led by Nicolai Ardoino, another veteran of 1849. These infantry units were supplemented by 50 scouts, or guides, which included Garibaldi's son Menotti, under Francesco Simonetta; plus 40 Genoese *carabinieri* (sharpshooters), a company of sappers, an ambulance company and a battery

Based on a photograph by Charles Marville, this engraving depicts Conte Camillo di Cavour, who was prime minister of the Kingdom of Piedmont-Sardinia during the Second War of Italian Independence. Cavour was anxious to ensure that Garibaldi's popularity did not eclipse his own efforts to establish a Kingdom of Northern Italy dominated by the House of Savoy. (Anne S. K. Brown Military Collection)

of mountain artillery, which arrived too late for use in the forthcoming campaign. Two regiments of chasseurs and a battalion of cadets was also organized, but too late in the war to see action. Although uniformed in the dark blue of the Piedmontese Army, many of these volunteers were poorly armed and equipped as they were considered an auxiliary force to the main army. Aware of this, Garibaldi wrote later: 'In 1859 I was kept as a flag to attract recruits … but to command only a small proportion of them, and those the least fit to bear arms.'

When the Austrians under Field Marshal Franz Joseph Gyulai, Governor of Lombardy-Venetia, invaded Piedmont by crossing the river Ticino in heavy rain on 29 April 1859, the Cacciatori delle Alpi were concentrated at Brusasco, near Turin, and were ordered to Casale to link up with the small Piedmontese Army. Meanwhile, France did not declare war until 3 May, and a French army of approximately 130,000 men under General Patrice de Mac-Mahon was slow to cross the Alps in order to link up with the Piedmontese. The Austrians failed to take advantage of this and, rather than sweeping forward around Turin to block the French advance, wasted time conducting reconnaissance in eastern Piedmont. Arriving at Casale with his command, Garibaldi found no orders waiting for him. After four frustrating days of inactivity he rode south to the King's headquarters at San Salvatore to request that his volunteer troops be taken more seriously, and on 9 May was given royal orders to operate against the Austrian right flank near Lake Maggiore at the foot of the Alps, where he had achieved minor victories 11 years before. No sooner had he led his command in the still-pouring rain towards Biella when these orders were countermanded by Cavour, who required Garibaldi to march his troops to Vercelli, west of Milan, where he was to place himself under the command of General De Sonnaz. Cavour was clearly making every effort to ensure that Garibaldi's republican zeal and popularity did not eclipse his own desire for the realization of a Kingdom of Northern Italy dominated by Piedmont.

Undeterred, Garibaldi obeyed orders and marched the Cacciatori to San Germano, only to discover that De Sonnaz was completely unprepared to move against the Austrians. Hence he withdrew and continued on his way to Biella where, just as Cavour feared, he was greeted enthusiastically. Four days later he led his troops down from the wooded hills towards Arona on the shore of Lake Maggiore. Instead of next marching north towards Meina, Garibaldi fooled the Austrians on the other side of the lake by moving south towards Castelletto, where the waters converge into the fast-flowing Ticino. Under cover of night, his troops crossed the wide river in barges commandeered several days before by Simonetta's guides. They became the first Piedmontese forces to invade Austrian-dominated Lombardy, and they captured the small garrison at Sesto Calende without firing a shot.

Published in Paris in 1860, this lithograph by H. Jannin shows Garibaldi wearing the dark-blue uniform of the commander of the Cacciatori delle Alpi, or Alpine Chasseurs, of the Piedmontese Army. (Anne S. K. Brown Military Collection)

The 1859 campaign

Map labels

SWITZERLAND

PARMA

LOMBARDY

PIEDMONT

VALTELLINA

N

Campaign routes of 1859

Napoleon III advances

Gyulai advances

20 miles

20km

Stelvio Pass (6)

Bormio

Tirano

Sondrio

Morbegno

Trento

Riva

Bezzecca

Lake Garda

Verona

Adige

Villafranca

Mantua

Peschiera

Custozzo

Lonato

Solferino

Salò

Tre Ponti

Castenedolo (5)

Chiese

Lovere

Iseo

Sarnico

Brescia

Oglio

Cremona

Piacenza

Trescore

Bergamo

Martinengo

Adda

Lecco

Monza

Milan

Pavia

Como (3)

Cameriata

Fino

San Fermo

Rovera

Olgiate

Malnate (4)

Cuvio

Gavirate

Varese

Varano

Sesto Calende

Castelletto (1)

Gallarate

Magenta

Urban (11,000) xx

Gyulai (238,000) xxxx

Ticino

Bellinzone

Locarno

Lugano

Lake Maggiore

Laveno

Meina

Arona

Domodossola

Varallo

Novara

Palestro

Vercelli

San Germano

Sesia

Casale

San Salvatore

Alessandria

Tortona

Tanaro

Po

Biella

Garibaldi (3,000) xx

Ivrea

Vittorio Emmanuele II (74,000) xxxx

Asti

Alba

Chivasso

Brusasco

Napoleon III (132,000) xxxx

Turin

(2)

Left: Not wishing to offend the more conservative Italian nationalists, the troops serving under Garibaldi in 1859 were not clothed in red shirts, which were usually associated with revolution. In this watercolour by Quinto Cenni, the Cacciatori delle Alpi are depicted wearing the black-trimmed grey uniforms issued later in the war. (Anne S. K. Brown Military Collection)

The battle of Varese

Within hours the Cacciatori were on the move again, marching north-east through Lombardy towards Varese. Occupying the town on 23 May 1859, they were attacked three days later by a 3,000-strong brigade of the Austrian Reserve Division under Field Marshal Karl Urban. However, Urban sent about a third of the Austrian infantry on a flanking movement to the right, which became lost in the hills, thus weakening his offensive. Preceded by an artillery bombardment, the Austrians drove in Garibaldi's outposts, only to be repulsed by the Cacciatori, who held their fire until the last minute and then rose from their defensive works, fixed bayonets and charged. According to English volunteer Frank Leward: 'They kept as quiet and firm as could be and not till the enemy was right on them and the word was given was a gun discharged. Then they gave it them well all round.'

Observing the enemy in retreat, Garibaldi ordered the brigade under Cosenz to turn the enemy's flank from the south. Riding up with his staff to address his advancing troops, he apologized for the fact that their breakfast had been disturbed and announced that it would be 'uncivil not to see [the Austrians] a little farther on their road after coming so far to visit us'. After advancing for several kilometres, the Cacciatori engaged with the Austrian rearguard near the village of San Salvatore, south-east of Malnate, and once again drove them back despite being outnumbered five to one. Becoming concerned that his troops might be cut off by the return of the Austrian flanking movement, Garibaldi ordered them back to Varese for the night.

Below: John Whitehead Peard fought for Italian unification in both 1859 and 1860. Painted by Thomas Nast, this watercolour was produced at Messina on 22 August 1860, two days before Peard resigned his commission with Medici in order to join Garibaldi in Calabria. (Anne S. K. Brown Military Collection)

Urban lost 22 dead and 62 wounded and captured, compared with only about ten Cacciatori killed and 75 wounded and missing.

Garibaldi next ordered a daring advance towards Como, where the Italian leader was hopeful of launching a surprise attack. Marching through Malnate towards Olgiate, he diverted his main force in a north-easterly direction at Solbiate towards the lightly guarded pass of San Fermo, leaving Cosenz's brigade to continue east towards the railhead at Camerlata, where Urban was concentrating his troops. On 27 May 1859 the Cacciatori arrived undetected at the head of the pass and, according to battalion commander Nino Bixio, 'cast themselves down like a torrent', driving back the small force of Hungarian infantry, as well as the Austrian reinforcements that came struggling up the slope from Como. Waiting until nightfall, Garibaldi ordered his troops to secure everything that might rattle and advance in complete silence down into the town. Unfortunately, as they reached the suburbs they were greeted loudly by the local residents.

But the Austrians had gone. Consisting of eight infantry battalions, plus artillery and Uhlans (lancers), they had been withdrawn in confusion by Urban about an hour before the Cacciatori entered the town, leaving behind his military chest plus a vast array of arms, equipment, money and rations. However, with the enemy still occupying Laveno on the shore of Lake Maggiore to the north-west, and with Urban's main force regrouping between Monza and Milan to the south-west, Garibaldi could not linger long in Como. After a day's rest, he marched towards Laveno, where the Austrians not only threatened his line of communications but were preventing Piedmontese regulars from crossing the lake. He arrived there on 30 May and organized a frontal attack as a diversion while his main force was sent to assault the town from the north. Unfortunately the flanking movement lost its way, and the frontal assault was repulsed with high casualties. Furious with his first major failure of the campaign, Garibaldi ordered a withdrawal. With Laveno still in enemy hands and with more Austrians approaching, the Cacciatori were in danger of being cut off. However, upon returning to Como, he learned that forces under Vittorio Emmanuele II had won an important victory at Palestro on the same day as his failure at Laveno, following which Urban was recalled south. Five days later, the French inflicted a punishing defeat on the Austrians at the battle of Magenta.

As a result, Garibaldi was able to continue operations with freedom. Proceeding east towards Lecco, he ferried the Cacciatori across the lake and then marched them south-east, entering Bergamo, then Brescia, where they were received with great public acclaim. Arriving at the city on 13 June 1859, he found new orders awaiting him. Cavour continued to be concerned about the success of Garibaldi's Lombardy campaign, and had ensured that the liberated territory was administered by officials favourable to Piedmont. He also deprived Garibaldi of his independent command and ordered him to advance on Lonato the next day with the promise of cavalry and artillery in support. Although they became involved in a fierce firefight with a much larger Austrian force at Castenedolo and suffered heavy casualties, the

Cacciatori remained unsupported and Garibaldi became convinced that this was a deliberate attempt by Cavour to get rid of him and his command.

Garibaldi was next ordered to march the Cacciatori north and far from the seat of war to the Stelvio Pass, which had been occupied by the Austrians on 18 June. By 27 June part of his force under Major Giacomo Medici had reached the Tonale Pass, and on 5 July he forced the Austrians to evacuate Bormio, close to the border with Switzerland. The following day he began the last action of the war when he attempted unsuccessfully to cross a glacier and negotiate rocky slopes to attack an Austrian blockhouse at Stelvio. Meanwhile, on 24 June, the French and Sardinian armies fought the bloody battle of Solferino which lasted over nine hours and resulted in more than 3,000 Austrian troops killed, 10,807 wounded and 8,638 missing or captured. In comparison, the Allied armies suffered a total of 2,492 killed, 12,512 wounded and 2,922 missing or captured. As a result, the Austrian army was forced to yield its position, and the Allied French–Italian forces won a tactical, but costly, victory. On 8 July 1859, the French and Austrian emperors met at Villafranca di Verona and, without consulting Vittorio Emmanuele II, signed an armistice, the terms of which were confirmed at Zurich in Switzerland on 10 November 1859. This brought the Second Italian War of Independence to a close.

Although deliberately sidelined from the main theatre of action by Cavour, Garibaldi and his Cacciatori delle Alpi had made a valuable contribution towards the course of this conflict by keeping over 11,000 Austrian troops occupied in the foothills of the Alps. Furthermore, Garibaldi had revived the worldwide reputation he had gained during the defence of the Roman Republic of 1849. He now looked to the future for a further opportunity to achieve the ultimate goal of the liberation and unification of the whole of Italy. He did not have to wait long.

The War of 1860

When he heard news of the armistice Cavour resigned in disgust, while Garibaldi accepted an invitation by Baron Bettino Ricasoli, one of the new moderate leaders in the Central Italian League, to join the army formed by the alliance of the Grand Duchy of Tuscany, the Duchies of Modena and Parma and the Romagna. Appointed as second in command of the Central States' army, under General Manfredo Fanti, he also became president of the reconstituted National Society, but resigned on 29 December 1859. Met with a hero's welcome wherever he went, and greeted now as 'the General', Garibaldi was urged by many to continue the revolution by advancing south into the Papal States to take advantage of the nationalist spirit before it cooled. Indeed, he was given permission by General Fanti to invade the Marche and Umbria in the event of a nationalist rising there. However, Fanti's determination not to initiate hostilities for fear of further Austrian intervention led to the resignation of Garibaldi from his post on 16 November 1859. Following this, Garibaldi was summoned back to Turin, where Vittorio Emmanuele II offered him a generalship in the Piedmontese Army, which he refused, and a shotgun from the royal collection, which he accepted. Garibaldi was also granted permission to commence the collection of contributions for a 'Million Rifles Fund', and to purchase arms on the condition that the Piedmontese government was advised where the weapons were stored.

On a personal level, Garibaldi next journeyed to Fino, near Como, where on 24 January 1860 he married Giuseppina Raimondi, the 17-year-old illegitimate daughter of a Lombard nobleman, whom he had met a few months earlier. Immediately after the wedding ceremony she informed him that she was pregnant with another man's child, which resulted in his swift departure for Genoa and thence back to Caprera.

On 24 March 1860 Nice and Savoy were officially ceded to France as a result of the agreement that had led to the Second Italian War of Independence. Outraged by news that he had been made a 'foreigner' in his own country, Garibaldi would not be reconciled by Vittorio Emmanuele II who, as King of Piedmont, Savoy and Sardinia, retorted that he had also lost 'the cradle of his family'. Encouraged by supporters in Nice, Garibaldi began to formulate a far-fetched plan to lead a raid on his birthplace. Aided by English adventurer Laurence Oliphant, he would take 200 men armed with weapons from the Million Rifles Fund, smash the ballot boxes and scatter the voting slips, making it necessary for the Government to hold a new ballot. However, the raid on Nice was abandoned when Garibaldi received word that a long-awaited revolt against the Bourbon regime of Francis II had begun in Palermo, Messina and Catania, in Sicily, on 4 April 1860. Although unsuccessful, as the insurgents led by Francesco Riso and his nobly born namesake Baron Riso were surrounded in the Gancia Convent and killed or captured after a fierce battle, the rising began a pattern of Sicilian resistance that stimulated Garibaldi's conquest of the Kingdom of the Two Sicilies during the following months.

Preparing the expedition

Based at the villa of Augusto Vecchi at Quarto, near Genoa, 'the General' and his followers watched and waited as events continued to unfold in Sicily. Bands of peasant rebels and bandits formed themselves into *squadre* (squads) and skirmished with Bourbon troops in the mountains and plains outside Palermo. Rumours of unrest continued as veteran revolutionary Rosolino Pilo returned to Western Sicily in the hope of keeping the spirit of rebellion alive. Meanwhile, Garibaldi was gathering a small army of volunteers in preparation for his invasion that became known as *i Mille*, or 'the Thousand', which in fact originally numbered over 1,100, and would increase to about 20,000 by the end of the campaign. Finally, on 29 April 1860, Garibaldi decided there was still sufficient unrest in Sicily to warrant an attack, and he announced to his lieutenants: 'let us start'.

As an ex-sailor, Nino Bixio was given the task of preparing the embarkation, while Agostino Bertani continued his work of enlisting volunteers. Garibaldi requested permission to recruit from the Cacciatori delle Alpi, which had been reorganized as the 46th Regiment in the Piedmontese Army, but Vittorio Emmanuele II refused as he had no desire to see his own defensive force weakened against any future Austrian attack. The force quickly assembled by Garibaldi included mechanics, students, civil servants, journalists, authors, university lecturers, painters, sculptors, barbers, cobblers, chemists, seamen, engineers, 100 doctors, 150 lawyers and one woman – Rosalia Montmasson, who was the mistress of Francesco Crispi and who served as a cook and washerwoman. Most of them came from northern Italy and in particular from the towns and cities of Milan, Bergamo, Brescia and Pavia. About 100 volunteers originated from Sicily and Naples, but only 11 were from Rome. By 5 May 'the Thousand' had assembled at Quarto in the grounds of the Palazzo Spinola, which stood between the villa owned by Vecchi and the sea. At 9.30pm that evening Garibaldi strode through their ranks towards the waiting steamships, *Lombardo* and *Piemonte*, and the embarkation began.

This watercolour by Quinto Cenni depicts Garibaldi leading his troops during the Sicilian campaign of 1860. (Anne S. K. Brown Military Collection)

The voyage south was interrupted by a planned stop at the Gulf of Talamone on the Tuscan coast, where a detachment of 60 men under Callimachus Zambianchi was landed to make a diversionary march on the Papal States via Orvieto and Perugia. Garibaldi also successfully managed to persuade the commander of the nearby fortress at Orbetello that his expedition was under secret orders from Cavour, and that he should provide weapons and ammunition, including two cannon. Furthermore, he spent time organizing 'the Thousand' into a functional military organization by having them instructed, albeit briefly, in the rudiments of drill with their smooth-bore muskets, most of which were converted flintlocks. All the infantry were formed into two battalions of four companies each, the first containing 500 men commanded by Bixio and the second, with 600 men, under the Sicilian Giacinto Carini. The remaining troops consisted of 43 men of the Genoese Carabiniers, which was the only elite force under Garibaldi's command, plus a few artillerists, scouts and headquarters staff.

With news of the sailing of Garibaldi's expeditionary force, Europe was in uproar. Prussia, Russia and Austria protested. France countermanded the proposed withdrawal of her troops from Rome. Britain expressed fear that France would be rewarded for her protection of Italy against Austria with the cession of Sardinia or Genoa to a new state. Concerned to preserve the alliance with France, Cavour felt obliged to issue orders demanding the arrest of the expedition if it entered a port in Sardinia. With fears of the consequences of Garibaldi's plan greatly increased as the *Lombardo* and *Piemonte* approached Sicily, Cavour next ordered that it be stopped 'at all costs'.

The landing at Marsala

Meanwhile, Garibaldi's expeditionary force was drawing close to the Sicilian coastline, where the warships of the Neapolitan Navy lay in waiting. He had at first intended to land near Palermo, the capital, but thinking it too dangerous with a large garrison there, had decided instead to make for a point farther along the coast south of Trapani. On the advice of Salvatore Castiglia, captain of the *Piemonte*, he eventually made landfall at Marsala, following a passage between the islands of Marettimo and Favignana. Although two vessels hove in sight as 'the Thousand' approached Marsala, they turned out to be the Royal Navy warships *Argus* and *Intrepid*, there to protect British interests in the harbour, particularly a shipment of wine and sulphur. Regarding the latter, the British government of Queen Victoria coveted control of Sicily's sulphur supply, at that time one of the most important sources of this useful mineral used for the manufacture of gunpowder. It was believed in London that the bureaucrats of the House of Savoy would be more amenable to a British sulphur monopoly than the Neapolitan administrators, and hence there was clandestine British support for Garibaldi's invasion.

Furthermore, some disloyal Neapolitan commanders had been plotting with foreign operatives since the death of the more decisive and strong-willed Ferdinando II, father of Francis II. Thus, further fears of discovery of the Marsala landings were allayed when the captain of a Sicilian fishing boat advised that the Neapolitan flotilla under Louis, Count of Aquilla, had sailed south-east towards Sciacca earlier that day. He also stated that the port had been left unguarded as the local garrison had marched for Palermo in the mistaken belief that the landing would take place there. Hence, on 11 May 1860, the two Piedmontese steamers rapidly approached the harbour at Marsala unopposed. Although the *Piemonte* got safely to the inner harbour, the *Lombardo* grounded in the entrance and hastily began to disembark its troops on the mole by the lighthouse via shore boats. In the meantime, the captain of the Neapolitan warship *Stromboli* had spied the landing activity, and had turned back to investigate. Although hastily advised by Commander Marryat, of HMS *Argus*, that British naval officers were ashore, and that British wine establishments might be in the line of fire, the *Stromboli* opened fire killing one civilian and wounding a volunteer helping to drag a gun ashore. With both Piedmontese vessels by then completely divested of men and stores, the Neapolitans succeeded in towing the *Piemonte* out to sea, while the *Lombardo* was scuttled, being stuck fast.

During the landing of 'the Thousand' at Marsala on 11 May 1860, the steamer *Piemonte* is seen in the foreground with the bow of the grounded *Lombarde* close behind. The two British warships *Argus* and *Intrepid* watch nearby. The Neapolitan warship *Stromboli* is shown in the distance. (Anne S. K. Brown Military Collection)

Following a disappointing reception from the local population at Marsala, who regarded the 'invaders' with suspicion, Garibaldi and his 'Thousand' began the march towards Palermo the next day, and were glad to be joined by the first of the bands of Sicilian *squadre*, also known as *picciotti* (meaning 'little fellows'), which they were dependent on in order to swell their ranks. Reaching the hill town of Salemi, Garibaldi proclaimed a dictatorship in the name of King Vittorio Emmanuele II, and announced the abolition of various unpopular taxes imposed by the Bourbons. The government established soon after was headed by Francesco Crispi, who would later become Italy's prime minister.

In the meantime, Neapolitan forces gathered in order to quell the new threat to their regime. With news of the landing at Marsala, the aged Governor of Sicily, Paolo Ruffo di Bagnaria, the Prince of Castelcicala, dispatched a column of about 3,000 troops from Palermo that made very slow progress, not reaching Calatafimi until 15 May, with the 70-year-old Brigadier-General Francisco Landi following behind in his carriage. At the junction of the roads from Trapani and Salemi, which then led to Palermo, Landi realized the strategic importance of Calatafimi and established his base of operations there. Hesitant with regard to strategy and anxious that his lines of communication with Palermo might be cut by the *squadre*, he contented himself with sending out small detachments of troops to scout and probe towards Salemi, 'to impose morally upon the enemy'. It was one of these detachments, consisting of a light infantry battalion of 600 men of the 8th Cacciatori under Lieutenant-Colonel Michele Sforza, that Garibaldi's troops encountered on the Piante di Romano, a high hill outside Calatafimi, that same day.

Calatafimi

Riding ahead of his column, which had rested overnight at Vita, Garibaldi ascended Monte Pietralunga and spied Sforza's light infantry on the Piante di Romano. He immediately ordered his troops to advance up from Vita to the slopes of the hill at his rear. Meanwhile, observing what he considered a rabble at his front, Sforza decided to ignore orders to avoid combat. To impress his enemy he put his men through a series of drill manoeuvres, which the *garibaldini* duly cheered, and then advanced his battalion down into the valley and up the long and difficult slope of Monte Pietralunga. While the *squadre* sheltered nervously either side of the road watching the approaching regular infantry, the poorly armed *garibaldini* gathered in two thin, ragged lines above them. As the Neapolitans drew near they fired by the volley with their percussion rifle muskets, only to be answered by the sporadic return fire of the grey-coated Genoese Carabiniers, who were the only Garibaldian troops armed with rifled weapons (in the form of Swiss carbines). With smoothbore muskets sighted to only 300m, and carrying only ten rounds of ammunition each, the remainder of 'the Thousand' were under orders to hold their fire and go in with the bayonet. The 5th, 6th and 7th Companies, with the flag, made up the front line. Behind them was Bixio's battalion, consisting of the 1st, 2nd, 3rd and 4th Companies.

Suddenly, and without orders, some of the *garibaldini* rushed down the hillside at their enemy and threw the Neapolitan skirmishers back across the valley to the foot of the Piante di Romano. Although encouraged by the covering fire of the Genoese Carabiniers, they lacked artillery support as their antiquated guns under Vincenzo Orsini had been forced behind a barricade on the Vita road by a squadron of Neapolitan Horse Chasseurs. Ascending the steep, terraced slope above them, the *garibaldini* sought refuge behind low stone walls as they came under fire from the main enemy force. Making short rushes from one terrace to the next, they approached ever nearer to the Neapolitan infantry, who tended to fire too high, missing their targets.

Although General Landi reinforced Sforza with five infantry companies and some cavalry from his reserve, he was concerned that the *squadre* lurking in the slopes might cut off his retreat from Calatafimi if he committed his whole force. They had already cut the electric telegraph and disrupted the semaphore system communicating with Palermo. It also appeared to him by mid-afternoon that Sforza's troops were holding their line and would not need further help, and that Garibaldi's men were wavering. Indeed, the latter were struggling under fire, and suffering from thirst and hunger under the relentless Sicilian sun. Many were wounded, and those who were able began struggling back to the safety of the valley below. In an effort to rally his troops, Garibaldi dismounted and, followed by his staff, walked down from the Monte Pietralunga with sword in hand to urge his men forward. At the same time, exposing himself to enemy fire, Bixio galloped along the lines on a white horse offering encouragement to the flagging troops, while Chief of Staff Giuseppe Sirtori reorganized their ranks. In the heat of battle, it became apparent to Garibaldi that this was an action he could not afford to lose. Thus, when some of his young troops began to waver and crowded around their commander urging him to order a retreat, he turned on them and replied angrily: 'Here we shall make Italy – or die!' Some accounts relate that even Bixio enjoined Garibaldi with the same advice, and was rebuked in a similar manner.

Moving in amongst his foremost troops, Garibaldi awaited the moment to launch a final assault. Meanwhile, Orsini's artillery managed to come into action, following the withdrawal of the enemy cavalry. Elevating the aim of his guns, he fired a few high-trajectory shots on to the Piante di Romano. Although they caused little physical damage, their psychological value was considerable as they lowered the morale of the Neapolitans at a critical moment in the battle. Furthermore, the

During the first clash with Neapolitan forces at Calatafimi, Sicily, on 15 May 1860, battalion commander Nino Bixio is believed to have advised his commander, 'General, I think we should retreat', to which Garibaldi responded angrily, 'Here we shall make Italy – or die!' (Anne S. K. Brown Military Collection)

reserve company of *garibaldini* under Giuseppe Dezza arrived as extra support, and Cairoli's 7th Company, together with some of the Sicilians, attacked the eastern side of the hill where the ascent was less steep.

By 3.00pm Garibaldi had gathered about 300 men around him ready for a final assault on the last of the terraces. Realizing that the enemy was throwing rocks because they were running out of ammunition, he seized the moment and rushed to the top of the hill waving his sword. Followed by his fiercely loyal legionaries, they were met with volley fire and a further hail of rocks. A desperate mêlée ensued, during which a burly Cacciatori sergeant snatched the Garibaldist flag (the Italian tricolour) from its staff, at the same time wounding Garibaldi's son Menotti, who was one of three young officers forming the colour guard. But soon the Neapolitans began to fall back down the hillside towards Calatafimi. Too exhausted to pursue them, the *garibaldini* began to regroup and take stock of their victory.

The Neapolitans had suffered about 120 casualties, including dead and wounded, while Garibaldi's losses were much heavier, amounting to 30 killed and 150 wounded. Included among the former were many teenage boys, the youngest of whom had just reached his 14th birthday. Nonetheless, the day belonged to Garibaldi and 'the Thousand'. Below in Calatafimi, General Landi attempted to send a dispatch to the Governor of Sicily claiming that he had killed Garibaldi, but also requesting 'Help! Prompt help!' This was captured en route and read with indignation and merriment. By midnight Landi had evacuated the town and his column was marching as fast as it could to Palermo via Alcamo and Partinico. Harried by the *squadre*, they burned and destroyed as they went.

The capture of Palermo

Garibaldi received a hero's welcome as he passed Alcamo, where many fell on their knees in worship as he passed by. Meanwhile, the *squadre* under Rosolino Pilo lit beacon fires along the crests of the mountains overlooking the Conca d'Oro, the plain surrounding Palermo, as a sign to the people that their liberators were approaching. Having reached the Renda plateau high above Palermo, 'the Thousand' next endured three days of rain without tents or any other form of shelter. Between them and Palermo stood Monreale, which was held by three battalions of Neapolitan infantry. A further 20,000 troops, plus several warships, also awaited them in Palermo. Well aware that he could never defeat such a powerful garrison on the battlefield, Garibaldi's only hope was to slip into the town at its weakest point with the help of the Sicilian guerrillas. Once inside Palermo, he hoped to spark off a revolution in the streets. But first the troops at Monreale had to be dealt with, and this duty he entrusted to veteran guerrilla Rosolino Pilo, whose *squadre* occupied the high ground at Sagana.

Published in the *Ueber Land und Meer*, of Stuttgart, this engraving shows the encampment of Garibaldi's army prior to the capture of Palermo in May 1860. By this time 'the Thousand' had been supplemented by about 2,000 *picciotti*, or Sicilian guerrillas. (Anne S. K. Brown Military Collection)

However, before he could carry out his orders, which were to seize the heights overlooking Monreale, Pilo was surprised by three columns of Neapolitan infantry that fell on his pickets, and who shot him as he took cover behind a rock to write a dispatch requesting reinforcements. This caused Garibaldi to change his plans and he decided instead to approach Palermo along the road from Parco (now known as Altofonte), where he joined forces with Giuseppe La Masa, leader of the popular insurrection of 1848, whose guerrilla band occupied Monte Grifone and a steep craggy spur called Cozzo di Crasto, which overlooked the whole area. La Masa agreed to fall on the enemy's flank as soon as the Neapolitans attacked. Following this Garibaldi would launch a frontal counter-attack. However, when two strong enemy columns converged on his position on 24 May, Garibaldi decided to withdraw rather than risk being surrounded, despite the fact that La Masa's flanking attack had already begun. Badly mauled by the disciplined Neapolitan musketry fire, the Sicilians were outraged when they saw the *garibaldini* disappearing down the mountainside to their rear. As he regrouped his men after being driven back, La Masa had great difficulty in preventing many of his force from abandoning the fight and going home. Even some of 'the Thousand' were disappointed with their commander's lack of fighting spirit and his two failed attempts to capture Palermo. The high spirits engendered by the victory at Calatafimi were dispelled and the feeling prevailed among the *garibaldini* that the revolution might be over.

Fortunately, the two Neapolitan columns did not press home their assault. The one that had marched out from Palermo withdrew to the coast without giving pursuit as 'the Thousand' retreated towards Piana dei Greci. Meanwhile, the other slow-moving column, under Swiss commander Johann Lucas von Mechel, one of the best officers in the Neapolitan Army, took the misleading advice of locals and marched in the wrong direction into the Sicilian hinterland. This gave Garibaldi time to reorganize his disgruntled forces. Having sent his artillery, together with the sick and wounded, south towards Corleone under an escort of *squadre*, he led his exhausted infantry several kilometres along the same road but, once again adopting the tactics he had so successfully employed in Umbria and Tuscany following the fall of Rome in 1849, and more recently during the Alpine campaign of 1859, he suddenly veered off the Corleone road and led his column across country towards Santa Cristina and Marineo. He then took them north towards Misilmeri, which was only 16km (10 miles) from Palermo. Once they were resting in that place by 25 May, he sent a message to La Masa's headquarters at Gibilrossa requesting a meeting with the guerrilla leader at 3.00am the following morning in order to 'make important arrangements'.

Based on advice given by Ferdinand Eber, a Hungarian by birth and correspondent for *The Times* in Italy, who visited his encampment, Garibaldi and his officers decided to attack Palermo under cover of night from the south-east via its weakest gate, the Porta Termini, following which they would rush to the unguarded centre of the city. As a result, it was hoped that the Neapolitans, whose main force was deployed at the western and southern approaches to Palermo, being firmly convinced that Garibaldi was still in retreat, would be taken unawares.

As the column marched quietly across the Conca d'Oro on the night of 26–27 May 1860, it was led by 50 well-armed skirmishers under the Hungarian Lajos Tüköry. Following behind was a swarm of about 3,000 guerrillas who carried blunderbusses and shotguns, plus pikes and scythes. Next came 'the Thousand', which by then numbered less than 750 men, who were ragged and exhausted after two weeks of campaigning and exposure. By the time they had reached Ciaculli, which was halfway between Gibilrossa and the outskirts of Palermo, the guerrillas had become noisy and excitable, and were thrown into panic by a bolting horse.

The noise created as they approached the long Ponte dell' Ammiraglio, or Admiral's Bridge, over the river Oreto, alerted the Neapolitans, and Tüköry's advance guard came under concentrated enemy fire. As the skirmishers threw themselves to the ground, the guerrillas behind them scampered back down the road and sought shelter in the vineyards, leaving Tüköry's men exposed and in danger of being cut off.

At that moment, Garibaldi once again displayed courage and decisive command skills. Shouting, 'Avanti! Avanti! Cacciatori! To the centre of the town', he encouraged Nino Bixio's battalion and the Genoese *carabinieri* forward along the road to join Tüköry, and they forced their way across the bridge. With their infantry scattering, a squadron of Neapolitan cavalry appeared farther along the riverbank, but, seeing the strength of the opposition, its commander ordered a withdrawal and it trotted away without firing a shot. With the road into Palermo now open, Garibaldi ordered a rapid advance of about 1.6km (1 mile) to the Porta Termini. Although the gate itself had been removed, the entrance was barricaded and the *garibaldini* were caught in an enfilading fire from Neapolitan infantry under General Bartolo Marra, which wounded many, including Tüköry and Bixio. Tüköry still managed to reach the barricade and was killed as he attempted to pull it down. Meanwhile, Garibaldi and several of his officers drove the *squadre* forward from the Ponte dell' Ammiraglio. As the greater weight of numbers arrived, the barricade gave way and the *garibaldini* scrambled over the wreckage and continued on towards the Fiera Vecchia, an old market place, where the revolution in 1848 had begun. Arriving there at about 4.00am accompanied by Bixio, who had by then cut from his chest the bullet which had wounded him at the Porta Termini, Garibaldi was surrounded by wildly cheering Palermitans.

As the *garibaldini* next began to spread through the labyrinth of narrow streets that formed the centre of Palermo, the guns aboard the Bourbon

During the attack on Palermo on the night of 26–27 May 1860, Garibaldi's column is shown forcing its way across the Ponte dell' Ammiraglio, or Admiral's Bridge, over the river Oreto. The Hungarian Lajos Tüköry is shown waving the flag at left, while Garibaldi is mounted at centre. Tüköry was wounded and killed soon afterwards while breaking down the barricade at the Porta Termini. (Anne S. K. Brown Military Collection) warships and the batteries in the citadel opened up a barrage of shot and shell on the congested city centre. Despite previous protests from John Goodwin, the British Consul, and Admiral Sir Rodney Mundy, who commanded the British Fleet in Sicilian waters, General Ferdinando Lanza, who had replaced General Landi, was prepared to endanger the lives of the civilian population of the city in order to repel what he considered to be 'foreign invaders'. Soon whole streets and alleyways were reduced to burning rubble and innocent Parlemitans were killed and maimed. Meanwhile, Neapolitan troops were ordered to sack and burn about 200 houses in the poorer quarter of the city, known as the Albergheria, killing countless additional civilians. This combined atrocity was entirely to the advantage of Garibaldi as it threw the previously uncommitted poor people unquestioningly onto his side. Such an ill-conceived tactic, which employed bombardment rather than the deployment of his 20,000 infantry to occupy buildings, also meant that Lanza lost an opportunity to surround and contain the centre of the insurrection, and gave Garibaldi time to occupy all the key points in Palermo. After two hours of bombardment and several more of plunder and arson, the Bourbon commander clearly thought he had done enough and ordered the guns to fall silent.

As a result, Garibaldi with his staff and about 30 *carabinieri* were able to advance as far north-west as the Quattro Cantoni, at the centre of Palermo. From there they turned west in the direction of the Royal Palace, driving the Neapolitan infantry under General Landi back from the Piazza Bologni. By noon Garibaldi was back at the Piazza Pretario, the administrative square of the capital, where he established his headquarters in the Senate House for the next three weeks. During the next 24 hours, the *garibaldini*, with continued support from the Palermitans, who threw boiling water and heavy household items on any Bourbon troops seen below their upper-storey windows, managed to push all the Neapolitan forces they encountered back into two strongholds called the Zecca and the Castellamare, on the seaward side of the city. About 18,000 Neapolitan troops had also become strongly entrenched around the cathedral and the Royal Palace. Hundreds more defended the barracks by the Vicaria Prison to the north. Furthermore, approaching the city from the south-west were columns of infantry from the garrisons at Monreale and Ponte Parco.

Meanwhile, the *garibaldini* had failed to capture many new weapons and were running out of shot and powder for the antiquated muskets they were using. However, this did not seem to dampen the spirits of their leader, and when he learned that the Neapolitans were advancing from the cathedral and were attempting to break through the Jesuits' College to the Piazza Bologni he immediately gathered some 50 men and charged towards the oncoming troops with such force that they were driven back to their defensive works around the cathedral. The bravery displayed by Garibaldi and the *squadre* in this minor action, and the lack of fighting spirit shown by the Neapolitan troops, convinced the aging General Lanza that the 'invaders' could not be defeated. Having sustained 800 men wounded and

Following clandestine British support during the campaign of 1860, Admiral Mundy bade farewell to Garibaldi aboard his flagship HMS *Hannibal* in the harbour at Naples. (Author's collection/ILN)

200 killed, he decided to end the fighting and requested a truce and conference aboard HMS *Hannibal*, flagship of Admiral Mundy.

Even news of the return of the troops under Mechel failed to alter his decision. Unaware that a truce had been requested, Mechel's column marched through the Porta Termini towards the Fiera Vecchia, initially scattering the few Sicilians behind their barricades. Rallied by Sirtori, Garibaldi's chief of staff, the *squadre* eventually managed to hold their ground and prevented any further Neapolitan advance. In the meantime, dressed in the uniform of a Piedmontese general, Garibaldi met with Generals Letizia and Chretien aboard HMS *Hannibal*, in the presence of Captain J. S. Palmer of the US frigate *Iroquois*, to arrange the truce. After fierce objections to the presence of foreign naval officers and an attempt to suggest that a petition should be organized to gauge the wishes of the citizens of Palermo, Letizia finally agreed to a ceasefire until noon the following day. This would permit the evacuation of the Neapolitan wounded from the cathedral and the free passage of provisions to it. Before he left, Garibaldi attempted unsuccessfully to purchase gunpowder off the American naval officer. With his small army nearly out of ammunition, he seriously contemplated a retreat across the Conca d'Oro to the mountains. However, as he returned to his headquarters he was greeted by a revolution in the streets of Palermo as the whole population seemed to have risen in support and was reinforcing the barricades and arming themselves with makeshift weapons. By the following morning, Lanza realized that events had overtaken him, and he cancelled his order for a full-scale attack to be made immediately after the truce had expired. Instead, he found himself asking for a further three days' armistice. In response, Garibaldi shrewdly demanded that the Neapolitans hand over the contents of the mint. Amounting to 134,000 ducats, this now assured that he could properly arm and equip his army. Finally, on 7 June 1860, Lanza admitted defeat and led his 20,000 troops out of Palermo and into a temporary encampment on the

Volunteers of the 'second expedition' aboard the *Washington* as it steams towards Palermo in June 1860. Known as 'Garibaldi's Englishman', John Whitehead Peard stands at right wearing a white havelock cover over his cap. Sat at extreme right is Garibaldi's American naval aide Captain William de Rohan, who purchased the three ships used to transport the troops. (Author's collection/ILN)

northern outskirts of the city. Manning the barricades, and at last wearing the red shirts that gave them distinction and authority, the remnants of 'the Thousand' possessed only 390 muskets between them. Owing to a shortage of naval transport, 12 days passed before the last Neapolitan troops were embarked and carried back to Naples.

Meanwhile, on 9 June a ship arrived in the harbour laden with arms and ammunition for 'the Thousand'. Nine days later Giacomo Medici arrived in the Gulf of Castellamare with the 'second expedition' of *garibaldini* aboard the steamers *Washington*, *Oregon* and *Franklin*. Among the 2,500 troops with Medici was the blue-coated 2nd Pavia Company, composed mostly of students from northern Italy, commanded by 'Garibaldi's Englishman', John Whitehead Peard, plus two other British soldiers of fortune, John Dunne and Percy Wyndham – both of whom would also play an important role in the remainder of the campaign of 1860.

Milazzo

Following his victory at Palermo, Garibaldi was intent on defeating the remaining Bourbon troops in Sicily and crossing the Straits of Messina to the Italian mainland, where he intended to capture Naples and defeat the Kingdom of the Two Sicilies. In his way were 18,000 Neapolitan troops at Messina under General Thomas von Clary, while 1,000 more were garrisoned at Milazzo. A further 2,000 and 500 men were based on the south-east coast at Siracusa and Augusta respectively. An army of 80,000 awaited him on the mainland. Undeterred by the odds, Garibaldi sent two columns of troops towards Catania on the east coast of Sicily in order to cut off the garrisons at Siracusa and Augusta. The column initially commanded by István Türr, and by fellow Hungarian Ferdinand Eber after Türr was taken ill, marched overland enlisting many recruits in the villages along the way. The column under Bixio passed through Corleone and reached the south coast, where it sailed from Licata to Terranova. From there it proceeded across country to Catania where it joined Eber's column towards the end of July. Following this, Garibaldi sent Medici with his main force

Opposite:

1 Garibaldi attacks Milazzo from three directions on 20 July 1860. The centre and right columns, led by Medici and Simonetta and Specchia respectively, push Bosco's Neapolitan riflemen back to a tunny-pickling factory near Milazzo harbour.

2 The left column under Malenchini is thrown back by Neapolitan artillery that sweeps the beach and coastal road.

3 In danger of being flanked on his left, Garibaldi leads forward Dunne's 'Anglo-Sicilian Battalion', which rallies the *garibaldini* and pushes forward to capture the Neapolitan cannon.

4 Garibaldi is involved in a mêlée with Neapolitan cavalry near the bridge about 200m from the town gate.

5 With the arrival of the ex-Neapolitan warship *Tüköry*, Garibaldi is rowed out to her and directs gunfire on the Neapolitan troops, forcing Bosco to withdraw his troops into the castle in Milazzo. At 4.00pm Garibaldi orders a general advance into Milazzo and barricades the streets.

6 Having made no preparations for a siege, and with his troops mutinous, Bosco capitulates on 24 July 1860.

The battle of Milazzo, 1860

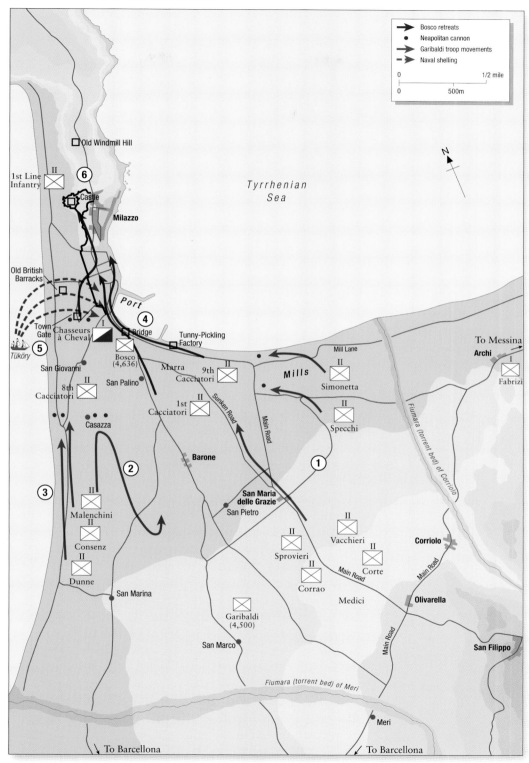

Legend:
- Bosco retreats
- Neapolitan cannon
- Garibaldi troop movements
- Naval shelling

0 — 1/2 mile
0 — 500m

Old Windmill Hill

1st Line Infantry

⑥

Castle
Milazzo

Tyrrhenian Sea

N

Old British Barracks

Port

Town Gate

Chasseurs à Cheval

④ Bridge

Tunny-Pickling Factory

Mill Lane

To Messina
Archi

Tüköry ⑤

San Giovanni

Bosco (4,636)

Marra

9th Cacciatori

II

Mills

II
Simonetta

I
Fabrizi

8th Cacciatori

II

San Palino

1st Cacciatori

Sunken Road

Specchi II

⑤

③

Casazza

②

Main Road

Barone

①

San Maria delle Grazie
San Pietro

II
Vacchieri

II
Corte

Corriolo

Malenchini II

Consenz II

Sprovieri II

Corrao II

Main Road

Medici

Main Road

Olivarella

Dunne II

San Marina

Garibaldi (4,500)

San Marco

Main Road

San Filippo

Fiumara (torrent bed) of Corriolo

Fiumara (torrent bed) of Meri

Meri

To Barcellona

To Barcellona

Sicilian skirmishers of the flanking column led by Colonel Malanchini are shown engaging with the advanced posts of Neapolitan infantry at Milazzo on 20 July 1860 in this engraving from the *Illustrated London News*. (Author's collection)

east along the north coast towards Milazzo, where Neapolitan troops under Colonel Ferdinand Benevento del Bosco awaited their approach at Barcellona. Skirmishing began on 17 July, and Bosco's troops were forced farther back towards Milazzo, where they continued to dig in. In response to Medici's request for reinforcements, Garibaldi dispatched a strong detachment under Enrico Cosenz, plus the so-called 'English Regiment' under Lieutenant-Colonel John Dunne. More commonly dubbed the 'Anglo-Sicilian Battalion', Dunne's command contained volunteers who had arrived from Britain for 'the love of Garibaldi', plus a number of British seamen who had 'deserted' ship to join the fray. The remainder of the rank and file of the battalion was mainly composed of young Palermitans, many of whom had been recruited from the 'Garibaldi Foundling Hospital' established in the city.

Garibaldi's plan was to attack Milazzo from three directions on 20 July. Veteran troops from Lombardy under Medici, composed of four battalions, formed the centre as they advanced along the main road from Meri. A flanking column under Colonel Malanchini, consisting of two battalions of Tuscans and a battalion of Palermitan recruits, attacked along the coast. Another flanking movement on the right, consisting of a single battalion of the 2nd Regiment, plus a battalion from St Lucia, led by Enrico Consenz, passed through Coriolo and approached from the east via the Messina road. A group of Sicilian *squadre* under Fabrizi took up a position on the extreme right to oppose any attempt by the Neapolitans to launch a counter-attack from Gesso, near Messina. Steady, if bloody, progress was made at the centre and on the right, where repeated charges by the *garibaldini* of the 'second expedition', anxious to prove they were as brave as the original 'Thousand', pushed the Neapolitans back to a tunny-pickling factory just outside Milazzo harbour. Unfortunately, the attack nearest the coast by Malanchini faltered and was thrown back as it became exposed to cannon fire sweeping the beach and coastal road.

Learning that Malanchini was in danger of being outflanked, Garibaldi led forward his reserve, which consisted of the 'Anglo-Sicilian Battalion' under Dunne, to stem the advancing enemy. His presence and the exertions of the English battalion officers, including Percy Wyndham, steadied the youthful volunteers, who not only resisted further attacks but pushed forward and captured two cannon. During a Neapolitan counter-attack, a detachment of the Chasseurs à Cheval charged amongst the *garibaldini* attempting to recapture the guns. Observing the action that followed, a London *Times* correspondent reported:

Garibaldi had only time to step aside when the horsemen passed, sabring [sic] right and left. But they did not go far, for after the first panic the infantry recovered and soon emptied the greater part of their saddles. The Captain, a sergeant, and a private tried to make their escape, and would have succeeded but for Garibaldi's personal bravery. He went into the middle of the road, and, having left his revolvers in the holsters when he dismounted, he drew his sword, and placed himself in a position to stop the Captain. The only person with him at that time was Captain [Giuseppe] Missori, of the Guides, who was likewise on foot, but armed with a revolver. His first shot, wounding the horse of the Neapolitan Captain, brought it on its haunches; Garibaldi seized hold of the bridle, intending to secure the Captain as his prisoner. But the Captain answered … by a blow with his sword at Garibaldi, who parried and retaliated, cutting the Neapolitan … with one stroke down the face and neck, and prostrating him dead at his feet. While Garibaldi was thus engaged in the single-handed combat, Captain Missori shot down the Sergeant who came to assist his officer. This one dispatched, he seized hold of the private whose horse had been shot, and, when he resisted, shot him also with another barrel of his revolver.

Withdrawing towards Milazzo, Bosco made another desperate stand by placing cannon either side of a bridge over a culvert 500m from the main gate of the town. Supported by the cannon in the castle on the rock behind town, and by riflemen either side of the road, he hoped to stem the flow of Garibaldi's advance. Losses were so great in front of this formidable position that Garibaldi wisely ordered his troops to dig in and hold, but not extend, their position. On his way across to the other beach to see what progress Consenz had made on the right flank, he spied a paddle steamer standing some way offshore south of Milazzo. Closer examination revealed this vessel to be the ten-gun *Tüköry*, formerly the *Veloce*, whose crew had deserted the Neapolitan Navy and had arrived to offer their services to the revolution. Commandeering a small boat, Garibaldi had himself rowed out to the *Tüköry* to request that the captain stand in closer to the shoreline in order to bombard the Neapolitan troops holding up his advance. With Garibaldi directing fire from the ship's rigging, the shot and shell went crashing into the Bourbon lines, forcing Bosco to finally order a withdrawal into Milazzo.

At 4.00pm Garibaldi ordered a general advance into the town, only to find that its streets were deserted and that Bosco had placed all of his exhausted and dispirited troops inside the castle on its granite precipice 90m (300ft) above the sea. It would not have been difficult to

This *Illustrated London News* engraving, based on a sketch by Thomas Nast, depicts the action at the bridge outside Milazzo. Note the British seamen, who were 'deserters' from the Royal Navy, kneeling firing at left. (Author's collection)

Based on a sketch by *Times* artist Frank Vizetelly, this coloured lithograph depicts the action near the bridge over a culvert outside Milazzo, Sicily, on 20 July 1860. Displaying typical personal bravery, Garibaldi is shown delivering a death blow to the Neapolitan cavalry captain, while aide Captain Missori, of the guides, shoots down two other men. (Anne S. K. Brown Military Collection)

defend such a formidable stronghold had the Bourbon commander had the foresight to bring in provisions while communications were still open. Fortunately for Garibaldi, he had failed to do so. By nightfall the *garibaldini* had barricaded the streets in case of a Neapolitan counter-attack. However, Bosco's troops were incapable of withstanding a siege, let alone organizing a counter-attack. With little food and no fresh water, they threatened to mutiny which left their commander with little choice but to ask for help. After exchanging semaphore messages with Clary at Messina, the latter relayed the bad news to Naples where, in the face of further mutiny in the Neapolitan navy, the ministers decided that both Milazzo and Messina should be surrendered.

Garibaldi and his lieutenants at Messina, 1860

In 1860 Garibaldi (**1**) was described by one of his officers as being 'of middle stature, with broad and square shoulders, herculean limbs, long brownish hair, and beard slightly gray; a heavy and strong step, sailor-like air and manner of speaking. The most characteristic part of his costume was the famous red shirt he wore in the Italian campaigns.' Hungarian exile István Türr (**2**) had fought under Garibaldi in 1859 and was badly wounded at Rezzato towards the end of that campaign. Completely recovered by the following year, he was a member of 'the Thousand' and subsequently commanded about 500 Hungarians, which made up the largest contingent of foreign volunteers fighting with Garibaldi in 1860. Giacomo Medici (**3**), the Marchese of Vascello, commanded the Students' Corps in 1849 and also served under Garibaldi in 1859. He sailed with the second Sicilian expedition and, after landing at the Gulf of Castellamare, took part in the remainder of the campaign. Commanding a battalion of the Cacciatori delle Alpi in 1859, Nino Bixio (**4**) helped organize the Sicilian expedition the following year. Adopted later in the 1860 campaign, he wears a hussar-style uniform with a red dolman and white pelisse. A Franciscan friar and revolutionary, Giovanni Pantaleo (**5**) became the chaplain of 'the Thousand' in Sicily and fought under Garibaldi in successive campaigns until 1871. He wears a red coat under his monk's habit, and 'top boots' or *Stulpenstiefel*.

This third consecutive victory for Garibaldi was costly, as he had sustained about 800 killed and wounded, which was over four times that of the Neapolitan Army. Arriving at Milazzo harbour aboard the *Fulminante* on 23 July, Colonel Anzani signed a treaty that resulted in the Bourbon troops evacuating the castle with their arms and half the battery mules. The artillery and ammunition, plus the remaining mules and the horses, were left behind. Virtually the last man to leave the castle, Bosco was hissed and jeered at by the townspeople as he made his way to the harbour. Five days later, General Clary reluctantly signed a treaty that provided for the complete suspension of hostilities, the occupation of Messina by the *garibaldini* and the withdrawal of Bourbon troops into the citadel there, where they were to remain passive spectators of further events.

Above: At the foot of the round tower of the castle at Milazzo, the Anglo-Sicilian Battalion exchanges fire with Neapolitan troops from behind a barricade across the street. Although both officers and enlisted men of this unit wore a jacket and trousers of unbleached white cloth, or *grezzo*, the lithographer has inaccurately chosen to colour their uniforms red. (Anne S. K. Brown Military Collection)

The conquest of Calabria

Following the victory at Milazzo, Cavour was determined to prevent Garibaldi from invading the Italian mainland. In a communiqué to Marquis Villamarina, Piedmontese chargé d'affaires in Naples, he advised that if that happened 'a revolutionary system' would take 'the place of the monarchist national party'. Remaining undisturbed by Cavour's machinations, Garibaldi continued to prepare his growing army to cross the Straits of Messina. Taking place during the night of 8 August 1860, his first attempt was a failure. After

Right: Following their victory at Milazzo, Garibaldi thanked the officers of the Anglo-Sicilian Battalion for their bravery in action. Hungarian revolutionary István Türr stands at his right. (Author's collection/IT)

rowing across in small boats and getting ashore undetected near Altifiumara, the hand-picked force of 200 men under Giuseppe Missori failed to capture Fort Torre de Cavallo, and were forced to retreat into the mountains. Ten days later, Garibaldi completely outwitted the Neapolitan Army and, with the assistance of British Royal Navy vessels, landed 6,000 volunteers at Melito on the south coast of Calabria. Despite rumours of the invasion, General Gallotti, the Neapolitan commander at Reggio, refused to order any of his troops south because he remained convinced that the main landing would occur somewhere along the west coast. This gave Garibaldi time to link up with Missori in the mountains. Shortly after midnight on 20 August he descended on Reggio and fought and won a bloody skirmish with Gallotti's troops in and around Piazza Duomo in the centre of the city, following which he captured the nearby castle, which served as the Neapolitan commander's headquarters.

The capture of Reggio was the first of a series of successes for Garibaldi in Calabria as the troops of the Neapolitan Army refused to fight and began to mutiny. On 22 August he marched north into the hills above Villa San Giovanni, where he joined forces with Cosenz, who had managed to get 1,300 men across the Strait from the lighthouse north of Messina while the Neapolitan fleet was off station making a belated attempt to prevent Garibaldi from landing at Melito. He captured the garrison at Villa San Giovanni on 23 August virtually without firing a shot. The following day the troops at Altifiumara surrendered unconditionally, followed by those at Torre Cavallo, and at the castle at Scilla. The cannon captured at these places were turned on the Neapolitan warships in the Strait, which enabled Medici to transport further fresh battalions from Messina.

Before the end of August, several thousand Calabrians had taken up arms in support of Garibaldi. Furthermore, Baron Stocco, one of 'the Thousand', had returned to his estate at Catanzaro and raised an additional 'army' of 6,000 farmers and peasants armed with shotguns and scythes, which was placed at the bridge over the river Angitola north of Pizzo to prevent the withdrawal of the remains of the Neapolitan Army from Monteleone to Naples. While General Vial escaped with a few men by boat from Pizzo, most of his remaining troops were left behind to make their way back to Naples overland as best they could. Fortunately for General Giuseppe Ghio, the guerrillas under Stocco permitted his troops to cross Lake Angitola under the mistaken belief that they had joined the revolution.

Meanwhile, Garibaldi quickened the pace of his advance in order to

Garibaldi steadies his telescope on the shoulder of a volunteer as he reconnoitres the coast of Calabria from Faro Point, in preparation for crossing the Straits of Messina to invade the Italian mainland. Fort Torre de Cavallo can be seen on the opposite shore in this *Illustrated London News* engraving. (Author's collection)

Above: On 30 August 1860
thousands of Neapolitan
troops under General
Giuseppe Ghio were
surrounded and persuaded
to capitulate at Soveria
Mannelli in Calabria.
Published in the *Illustrated
London News*, this
engraving shows at centre
John Whitehead Peard and
Irish artillerist Dick
Dowling, who entered the
village ahead of the main
garibaldini force.
(Author's collection)

prevent Ghio's troops from uniting with Neapolitan forces in Upper Calabria. Well in advance of his main column, and accompanied by his staff plus some British 'soldiers of fortune', which included John Whitehead Peard, he finally caught up with Ghio at Soveria Mannelli, a village high in the Calabrian mountains. On 30 August Peard approached Ghio's demoralized soldiers accompanied only by Irishman Dick Dowling, who commanded Garibaldi's artillery, and demanded their surrender, advising them that they were surrounded by *garibaldini*. Seeing both Stocco's guerrillas and Garibaldi's battalions closing in on him from the surrounding hills shortly after, Ghio agreed to capitulate, provided that his men were allowed to retire safely to their homes. Thus the last main Neapolitan force between that place and Naples evaporated.

About a week later, Peard was again greatly influential in hastening Garibaldi's advance. Constantly mistaken for 'the Dictator' himself because of his thick beard, military bearing and fluent Italian, he was greeted by liberated Italians with much kissing of hands and ringing of church bells. Taking advantage of this, he commandeered the telegraph office at Eboli, about 65km (40 miles) from Naples, and pretended to be Garibaldi as he sent messages to General Scotti, the Neapolitan commander at the capital, stating that his remaining forces had deserted and that *garibaldini* landings were expected at Salerno and in the Bay of Naples by 5.00am the next day. Incredibly, this telegraphic warfare worked. The Neapolitan commander panicked and began a military withdrawal from Naples. Entering Salerno as a conquering hero, Peard kept up the masquerade and appeared repeatedly on the mayor's balcony before cheering crowds. When he finally arrived in Salerno, the real Garibaldi stepped down from his carriage, swept off his hat and, advancing towards Peard, exclaimed: '*Viva Garibaldi*! So, you have stolen my name again.'

On 4 September 1860 King Francis II reluctantly decided to abdicate and escaped by steamer, allowing Garibaldi to enter Naples three days later as 'the Dictator' amidst wild celebration. With elements of the Neapolitan Army still in possession of the region north of the capital, the fighting was not over. Over 40,000 Bourbon troops occupied a position of great natural strength in an area that remained loyal to Francis II. The latter took refuge in the powerful fortress of Gaeta, midway between Rome and Naples, while farther south in Capua, protected by a fortress designed by Vauban, Field Marshal Joseph Ritucci reorganized the Neapolitan force of 50,000 men along the north bank of the river Volturno. Meanwhile, Garibaldi concentrated his troops at Caserta and, prior to making a fleeting return to Sicily, ordered a small force of about 200 men to cross the Volturno to disrupt Bourbon communications beyond Capua. He also hoped to deter Ritucci from launching a full-scale attack, which his volunteer army might find difficult to contend with. On his return on 19 September he found that Türr had extended this operation, having ordered the capture of the hill town of Caiazzo, plus a diversionary attack on Capua. Suffering the only defeat of the 1860 campaign, the *garibaldini* were repulsed at Capua with a loss of about 130 men killed and wounded.

The battle of Volturno

The Bourbon victory against the revolutionary forces gave Ritucci the boost he needed to launch a larger-scale attack. Furthermore, news arrived that Cavour had decided to stop Garibaldi's advance northwards, which might result in a war with France, by invading the Papal provinces of Umbria and Marche. This convinced the Neapolitan commander that it was essential that the forces of Francis II return to Naples before the arrival of those of Vittorio Emmanuele II, which were already marching south. Had Ritucci attacked on 22 September there is little doubt that he would have succeeded in breaking through to Naples. Apart from sandbag batteries in front of Sant' Angelo and Santa Maria and a flimsy breastwork linking the Porta Capua in Santa Maria with the amphitheatre, few revolutionary defensive works existed.

However, Ritucci reluctantly acted on the orders of the King's ministers at Gaeta, and sent one column of about 8,000 men under Mechel to protect his rear and left flank from attack by Garibaldian supporters in Piedimonte and Roccaromana. After a delay of about five days these troops approached Caserta from the south-west via Maddaloni. Meanwhile, the column under Ritucci prepared to advance on Caserta from the north-west. With no communication between these two forces, the Bourbons missed a valuable opportunity to launch a coordinated attack on Garibaldi's smaller army on 27 September. By the end of the month the revolutionary army of about 20,000 had been well placed with numerous entrenched batteries, and with Bixio on the right near Maddaloni, Medici on the left around Sant' Angelo and Santa Maria and Türr in reserve at Caserta. The easy movement of all these troops was facilitated by the railway line that ran from Capua to Naples.

Ritucci's main attack finally began at dawn on 1 October 1860, when he ordered his troops to approach Santa Maria along sunken lanes well screened by brushwood. Rushing at the defences at Santa Maria, they forced the ill-trained Garibaldian levies out of their defensive works. With great tactical skill, Garibaldi responded quickly by ordering Türr to send forward reserves by train from Caserta, which prevented a major Neapolitan breakthrough.

Greeted with wild celebration when he arrived in Naples on 7 September 1860, Garibaldi is shown calmly doffing his Calabrian hat as his carriage drives along the Strada di Toledo in this *Illustrated London News* engraving based on a sketch by Thomas Nast. (Author's collection)

Above: In this fanciful *Illustrated London News* engraving, Neapolitan troops are shown using a sunken lane to launch an attack on Garibaldi's lines during the battle of Volturno on 1 October 1860. (Author's collection)

Above right: Garibaldi leads a bayonet charge on the Neapolitan forces at Sant' Angelo during the closing stages of the battle of Volturno on 1 October 1860. (Anne S. K. Brown Military Collection)

Leaving that sector of the battlefield, he moved next to Sant' Angelo, where he believed the main attack would come. On the way his carriage came under fire. With his driver wounded and one of the horses dead, the vehicle ground to a halt. Waiting only to be joined by a few infantrymen from Sant' Angelo, Garibaldi jumped into the road, drew his sword and drove off the startled Neapolitan riflemen. This was the first of numerous charges led personally by Garibaldi that day, as he formed and re-formed his infantry, urging them forward, issuing orders and shouting encouragement with an energy normally beyond that of a 53-year-old suffering from arthritis. Despite this, it was difficult to see any signs of victory as the Bourbon troops continued to advance from the north-west and south-east. Ultimately, Garibaldi's victory that day was as much the result of the mistakes of the enemy as his own personal courage and command skills.

Approaching from the south-east via Maddaloni, Mechel chose to divide his force, attacking Bixio's 5,600 men with about only 3,000 Swiss mercenaries, and sending his subordinate, Colonel Giuseppe Ruiz de Ballesteros, with 5,000 Bavarian troops but no clear orders, around his right flank passing through the mountains via Limatola. His hope was that Ruiz

Opposite:

1. Ritucci sends a column under Mechel north to protect his rear and left flank from attack by Garibaldian supporters in Piedimonte and Roccaromana. After a delay of about five days these troops approach Caserta from the south-west via Maddaloni.
2. Ritucci's main attack finally begins at dawn on 1 October 1860, when he orders his 1st and 2nd Divisions to advance on Santa Maria along sunken lanes well screened with brushwood. Rushing at the defences at Santa Maria, they force the *garibaldini* out of their defensive works.
3. Able to respond quickly as he is close by, Garibaldi orders Türr to send forward reserves by train from Caserta, which prevent a major breakthrough.
4. Approaching from the south-east via Maddaloni, Mechel divides his force, attacking Bixio with 3,000 Swiss mercenaries and sending Ruiz de Ballesteros with 5,000 Bavarian troops to seize and occupy Old Caserta and to establish and maintain communications with the left and right flanks of the Bourbon army.
5. Showing little initiative, Ruiz turns aside to attack 300 men of Bronzetti's Bersaglieri battalion defending Castel Morrone. Capturing that place after a four-hour assault, he fails to advance farther, although Garibaldi's headquarters and rear now lay open to him.
6. Failing to dislodge Bixio's division with his smaller force, Mechel has no choice but to withdraw south-west towards Ducenta.
7. At about 3.00pm Garibaldi orders all his remaining reserves towards Santa Maria, and issues the message 'Victory along all the Line', following which he leads a bayonet charge towards Sant' Angelo. At about the same time, Eber leads a charge towards Sant' Angelo from the south-east across the Ciccarelli bridge. In danger of being cut off, Ricutti orders a general withdrawal. By 8.00pm all the Bourbon troops south of the Volturno, except Ruiz's 5,000 at Old Caserta, have been withdrawn into Capua. Most of those under Ruiz withdraw the next day.

The battle of Volturno, 1 October 1860

To Benevento

Dugenta
Mechel
Cantinella

Mechel

Mechel

Mount Longano

Arches of the Valley

Eberhardt
18

Ruiz
Mechel
Limatola

Toroni

Castell Morrone
Pianelli

Mount Virgo ·607

Lupara Range

Old Caserta

Sitazzi
18

Dezza
18

Fabrizi
18

Bixio
xx

Maddaloni

Ferry of Limatola
Ferry of Cajazzo

Volturno

Sacchi
Bronzetti
15

Railroad to Naples

San Nicholas la Strada

Türr
xx

Garibaldi (20,000)
XXXX

San Leucio

Caserta

Palace Garden
Royal Palace

Sacchi
15

Milano
15

Marcianise

Mount Tifata ·602

Medici
xx

Eber
15

Simonetta
17

San Prisco

Casapulla

San Tammaro

Dunne
17

Spangaro
17

Santa Maria (Old Capua)

Assanti
16

Malenchini
16

Miblitz
xx

Ferry of Trifisco

Afan de Rivera
1

Polizzy
1
1

Barbalonga

Marulli
2

Malenchini
16

La Masa
16

Vitulazio
Bellona

Capua
bridge

d'Orgemont
2

San Tammaro

Tabacchi
2

Casino Reale

To Teano

Foresta

N

Rittucci (28,000)
XXXX
1

Routes of Garibaldi attacks
Garibaldi positions 1 Oct 1860
Routes of Ritucci attacks
Ritucci positions 1 Oct 1860

0   2km
0   2 miles

49

Published in *Illustrirte Zeitung* of Stuttgart, on 1 December 1860, this engraving illustrates the historic handshake between Garibaldi and Vittorio Emmanuele II, who would soon be proclaimed first King of Italy by the newly constituted Italian parliament. The meeting took place in Teano, near Caserta, on 26 October 1860. (Anne S. K. Brown Military Collection)

would sweep down from Monte Caro on Bixio's left to support the frontal attack of the Swiss troops. However, the only instructions he gave Ruiz were to seize and occupy Old Caserta and to establish and maintain communications with the left and right flanks of the Neapolitan Army. An unimaginative commander who showed little initiative, Ruiz turned aside to attack a battalion of about 300 Bersaglieri under Pilade Bronzetti defending the medieval ruins of Castel Morrone. Capturing that place after a four-hour assault, he stayed there despite the fact that Garibaldi's headquarters and rear now lay open to him, while Mechel attempted unsuccessfully to dislodge Bixio's lines with his smaller force. By noon, the Swiss general had given up hope of reinforcement and withdrew south-west to Ducenta, realizing that Ruiz was not going to come to his aid. Meanwhile, Garibaldi's forces suffered heavy losses, particularly in Santa Maria where the town band endeavoured to encourage the defenders by playing with loud and remorseless determination in the main street. By 3.00pm all the remaining reserves from Caserta had been brought up by Türr, only to find almost 600 of their comrades lying dead or dying in the narrow streets of Santa Maria, which was by then almost surrounded.

Garibaldi chose this point to spread a message among his troops: 'Victory along all the Line.' Realizing that this had lifted the spirits of his troops, and recognizing once again a turning point in battle, he ordered Türr's reserves to fix bayonets and follow him in a charge out of Santa Maria towards Sant' Angelo in order to relieve the pressure on Caserta. At about the same time, former *Times* correspondent Ferdinand Eber, who was by then a colonel in Garibaldi's army, led a charge towards Sant' Angelo from the south-west across the Ciccarelli bridge. In danger of being cut off from his supply lines, Ricutti had no choice but to order a general withdrawal north of the Volturno. By 8.00pm all his troops, except Ruiz's 5,000 at Old Caserta, had been withdrawn into Capua. Learning the fate of the rest of the Neapolitans, Ruiz also retreated across the river the next day. Not including 2,253 prisoners of war, the Bourbons listed 991 killed and wounded. In comparison, the Garibaldians lost over 2,000 killed, wounded and missing. Despite the heavy losses, Garibaldi had proved capable of fighting and winning a large-scale pitched battle, albeit against an inefficient foe. Following his success at the Volturno, he met with Vittorio Emmanuele II at Teano on 26 October and greeted him as King of Italy. Following the annexation of southern Italy on 8 November, Garibaldi retired to Caprera, refusing to accept any reward for his services.

LATER YEARS, 1861–82

At the outbreak of the American Civil War in April 1861 Garibaldi volunteered his services to President Abraham Lincoln, and was offered a major-general's commission in the US Army, but his insistence that the war's main objective should be the abolition of slavery was unacceptable to the Lincoln administration at that time, while his insistence on being appointed commander-in-chief was unrealistic.

Following the issuance of the Emancipation Proclamation on 1 January 1863, Garibaldi wrote to Lincoln: 'Posterity will call you the great emancipator, a more enviable title than any crown could be, and greater than any merely mundane treasure.' Although he believed his place was in the 'field of action' rather than 'the parliamentary benches', Garibaldi accepted a seat in the Italian government when he was elected to the Chamber of Deputies in 1861. However, a violent outburst in the Chamber between Garibaldi and Cavour would have led to a duel with General Enrico Cialdini but for the intervention of the King.

Above: King of Piedmont, Savoy, and Sardinia from 1849 to 1861, Vittorio Emmanuele II became the first king of a united Italy on 17 March 1861 thanks to the successful military campaigning of Garibaldi. (Author's collection)

Having established the International Legion on 5 October 1860, Garibaldi continued the struggle not only for the unification of Italy but for all other European nationalities. With the motto, 'Free from the Alps to the Adriatic', the movement more immediately set its sights on Rome and Venice. Frustrated by the inactivity of the King, Garibaldi organized a new venture to attack the Papal States. Any challenge to the temporal domain of the Pope was bound to cause alarm among Catholics worldwide, and Napoleon III had guaranteed the independence of Rome from Italy by stationing a French garrison there. Although Vittorio Emmanuele II discouraged his subjects from participating in revolutionary ventures against the Pope's rule, Garibaldi believed he had the secret support of his government. In June 1862, he sailed from Genoa to Palermo, where he recruited volunteers for the impending campaign under the slogan *Roma o Morte* ('Rome or Death'). Gathering about 2,000 men, he attempted once again to cross to the mainland via Messina, only to have his passage barred by the King's orders. Turning south, he set sail from Catania, declaring that he would enter Rome as a victor or die beneath its walls. He landed at Melito on 14 August 1863 and marched at once into the Aspromonte, the mountains overlooking the Strait of Messina. Determined to prevent Garibaldi from reaching Rome, General Cialdini dispatched a division of regulars under Colonel Pallavicino, and the two forces met on 28 August. Although he forbade his men from firing on fellow subjects of the kingdom

Below: Captured at Aspromonte on 29 August 1862, these red-shirted Garibaldian troops are being conducted to the forts of Genoa. (Anne S. K. Brown Military Collection)

Leading another attempt to capture Rome, Garibaldi is shown surrounded by his legionaries, having been wounded in the foot near Messina on 14 August 1863. (Anne S. K. Brown Military Collection)

of Italy, the King's soldiers opened fire and a stray shot wounded Garibaldi in the foot. Taken prisoner along with several of his supporters, a government steamer took him to Varignano, where he was placed under house arrest and underwent painful treatment for his wound. Although this venture had failed, he received much sympathy and support for his cause across Europe, and was allowed to return to Caprera to recuperate.

In 1866 Garibaldi received the full support of the Italian government when he again took up arms. The Austro-Prussian War had begun and Italy formed an alliance with Prussia against Austria-Hungary in the hope of removing Venetia from Austrian rule in what became known as the Third Italian War of Independence. Garibaldi again gathered his Cacciatori delle Alpi, by then about 40,000 strong, and led them into Trentino, where he defeated the Austrians at Bezzecca on 21 July 1866, thus securing the only Italian victory in that war. During this action the Austrians, commanded by Generalmajor Franz Freiherr von Kuhn, captured Bezzecca, and the Italians fought desperately to recover it. Transported around the battlefield in a carriage, as he was still recovering from the wound received in 1863, Garibaldi was in danger of being captured on several occasions. However, the Italian artillery captured a hill close to the town and an infantry assault forced the Austrians to withdraw to their

The battle of Volturno, 1860

By about 3.00pm on 1 October 1860 Garibaldi had committed all his remaining reserves into battle, and still the Neapolitan right flank, consisting of troops under Colonels d'Orgemont and Marulli, continued to push forward. According to an eyewitness account, 'matters were beginning to look black, indeed, for the national cause, when Garibaldi, seeing how critical was the state of affairs, galloped to the head of three or four hundred of his men, and, shouting 'Corragio Avant!' dashed right into the enemy's ranks, and being followed by his soldiers, the royalists were driven back at the bayonet's point to the gates of Capua. This brilliant incident, which occurred at the foot of Monte St. Angelo, decided the fortunes of the day.' The Garibaldian volunteers wear various patterns of the famous red shirt, with a mixture of headgear consisting of black hats and red caps. The Neapolitan troops consist of elements of the 1st Guard Grenadier Regiment and 9th Puglia Line Infantry, and wear fatigue caps and either greatcoats or the *bigia* (jacket), with branch-of-service trim.

strongpoints in the surrounding mountains, thus marking a victory that cost over 500 Italians killed and wounded compared with 3,500 Austrian casualties. Regardless of this success, the Italian regular forces were defeated at sea and made little progress on land after the disaster of Custoza. Ultimately an armistice was signed by which Austria ceded Mantua and Venice to Italy, but this result was largely due to the military success of Prussia on the northern front, particularly at Königgrätz on 3 July 1866.

Following the creation of the Italian Volunteer Corps on 16 May 1866, Garibaldian volunteers gathered in the Piazza dell' Indipendenza in Florence, then the capital of Italy, in anticipation of the upcoming war against the Austro-Hungarian Empire for the control of north-eastern Italy. (Anne S. K. Brown Military Collection)

In 1867 Garibaldi strengthened his long-term ties with the Freemasons when he was elected Honorary Grand Master of the Grand Orient of Italy. He also continued to agitate for the capture of Rome and again marched on that city, but the Papal Army, supported by a French auxiliary force, proved more than a match for his badly armed volunteers. Wounded in the leg during the battle of Mentana on 3 November, he had to withdraw from papal territory. Following further imprisonment by the Italian government, he was again returned to Caprera.

When the Franco-Prussian War began in July 1870, Italian public opinion heavily favoured the Prussians, and many Italians attempted to enlist as volunteers at the Prussian embassy in Florence. Following the recall of the French garrison from Rome, an Italian Army under General Raffaele Cadorna captured the city on 20 September 1870. Rome was annexed to

Fought during the Italian offensive against the Austrians in the Trentino in north-eastern Italy, the battle of Bezzecca was a costly victory for Garibaldi on 21 July 1866. (Author's collection/ILN)

the Kingdom of Italy after a plebiscite held on 2 October, and a week later the results of this were accepted by decree.

All that Garibaldi had striven for concerning Italy had been achieved, yet his restless desire for freedom and equality throughout the world remained unabated. Like many other Italians he reversed his opinion of the French and, in September 1870, offered his services to the newly proclaimed Third Republic when Otto von Bismarck demanded the cession of Alsace and part of Lorraine, insisting that it was needed as a defensive barrier for the newly emerging German Empire. Garibaldi was given command of the Army of the Vosges, a French force that grew to about 15,000 multi-national volunteers, including his two sons, Menotti and Ricciotti, who served as officers. He fought an unimpressive campaign around Dijon which did little to prevent a French defeat in 1871. Following this he was elected to serve in the National Assembly of Dijon, but resigned his seat and returned to Italy after he was shouted down when attempting to speak at the first meeting.

Using Freemasonry as a vehicle, Garibaldi devoted much of the last 20 years of his life to a political plan to spread international freedom and equality. In 1879 he founded the 'League of Democracy', which advocated universal suffrage, the abolition of ecclesiastical property and

Above: French auxiliary troops, armed with the Chassepot rifle, fire into the poorly armed red shirts defending the fortified village at Mentana on 3 November 1867 during a failed attempt to capture Rome. Garibaldi was wounded in the leg during this action. (Anne S. K. Brown Military Collection)

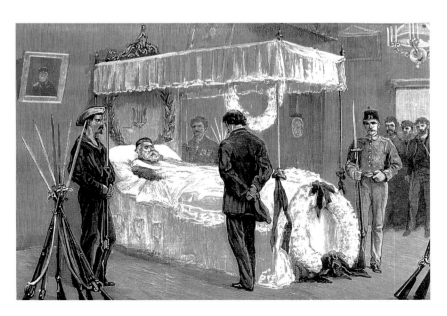

Left: Published in the *Illustrated London News* on 17 June 1882, this engraving shows the body of Garibaldi lying in state at Caprera after his death. (Anne S. K. Brown Military Collection)

the emancipation of women. Despite being elected again to the Italian parliament, he found his liberal ideals at constant odds with his reactionary fellow deputies, and spent much of his later years in Caprera. Although unwell and continuing to suffer from arthritis, he continued to make trips to Calabria and Sicily. In 1880 he married Francesca Armosino, with whom he had previously had three children. During his last days Garibaldi requested that his bed be moved to a window where he could gaze out to sea, where much of his life had been spent. He died on 2 June 1882 aged 74 and, against his wishes as a Freemason that his remains should be cremated, was buried on his farm on the island of Caprera alongside his last wife and some of his children.

OPPOSING COMMANDERS

The second Duc de Reggio, and eldest son of Napoleon Bonaparte's Marshal of France Nicolas Oudinot by his first marriage to Charlotte Derlin, **Lieutenant-General Charles Nicolas Victor Oudinot** (1791–1863) commanded the French army sent to crush the short-lived revolutionary Roman Republic and re-establish the temporal power of Pope Pius IX in 1849. Oudinot had served through the later campaigns of Napoleon Bonaparte from 1809 to 1814, and was promoted to major of cavalry in 1814 for gallant conduct. Following retirement during the early years of the restoration of the Bourbon monarchy under Louis XVIII, he was appointed superintendent of the cavalry school at Saumur and inspector-general of cavalry. Although 58 years old, he commanded with great vigour the French expedition sent to Italy in 1849. Surprised by the resistance he met when his troops attempted to enter Rome on 30 April, much of Oudinot's subsequent progress during the ensuing siege was due to the engineering skills of Lieutenant-General Jean-Baptiste Philibert Vaillant. After violating the terms of the armistice signed by the French in May 1849, Oudinot's renewed offensive finally defeated the exhausted Roman Republic and forced Garibaldi to abandon Rome. After the *coup d'état* of Louis Napoleon on 2 December 1851, Oudinot retired from military and political life. His brief account of the 1849 campaign was published in 1866.

Entering the French Army as an officer in the corps of engineers in 1809, **Jean-Baptiste Philibert Vaillant**, 1st Comte Vaillant (1790–1872), conducted the siege operations against Rome with great skill in 1849. Born in Dijon, he had served in the Russian campaign of 1812, becoming a prisoner of war after the battle of Kulm the next year. During Napoleon Bonaparte's Hundred Days, Vaillant fought at Ligny and Waterloo, and was wounded during the defence of Paris. Commanding a battalion in the 1830 campaign against Algiers, he was promoted to lieutenant-colonel and served under General Étienne Maurice Gérard during the Belgian campaign of 1831. He commanded the fortress at Algiers from 1837 to 1838, following

A skilful engineering officer, General Jean-Baptiste Philibert Vaillant, 1st Comte Vaillant, successfully conducted the siege operations against Rome in 1849. (Anne S. K. Brown Military Collection)

which he was recalled to France, where he was made director of the École Polytechnique. Promoted to lieutenant-general, Vaillant was placed in charge of the building of the Parisian fortifications in 1845 under the command of Inspector General Dode de la Brunerie. Following his success in Italy in 1849, he was made a Marshal of France in 1851, and served as minister of war from 1854 to 1859, holding the latter position throughout the Crimean War. In 1860 he was appointed as the minister responsible for the Imperial House and four years later was made grand chancellor of the Légion d'Honneur. After the fall of the second empire in September 1870 Vaillant was banished from France, but was permitted to return in 1871. He died in Paris the following year.

Above: A Hungarian nobleman who served as Austrian Governor of Lombardy-Venetia in 1859, Field Marshal Franz Gyulai was in overall command of the Austrian troops fighting Garibaldi in 1859. (Anne S. K. Brown Military Collection)

Commanding Austrian forces opposing Garibaldi during the Second Italian War of Independence in 1859, **Franz Joseph Gyulai** (1798–1868) was born in Pest, Hungary, to parents Ignaz Gyulai von Máros-Nemeth und Nádaska and Maria Freiin von Edelsheim. His father became a much-decorated general in the Austro-Hungarian Army during the Napoleonic Wars, and served as the Ban of Croatia from 1806 to 1831. In 1849 Franz Gyulai was named Austrian minister of defence by Emperor Franz Joseph, but served only one year. Upon the retirement of Joseph Radetzky in 1857 he was appointed governor of Lombardy-Venetia, residing at Milan. A field marshal at the commencement of war in 1859, he was unable to take advantage of the slow progress made by French troops during their entrance into the war. Thus, a crucial two-week delay allowed the forces of General Patrice de Mac-Mahon to come to the aid of their Piedmontese allies. Miscalculating that the Franco-Piedmontese attack would come from the south via Piacenza, Gyulai suffered a series of defeats at Montebello, Palestro and finally Magenta, on 4 June 1859. He was recalled to Vienna after his poor handling of his troops and, assisted by Feldzeugmeister Hess, Franz Joseph took command of operations himself. Reduced to a regimental commander, Gyulai surrendered the garrison at Mantua, one of the last fortresses to be incorporated into a united Italy in 1866.

A Sicilian by birth, **Ferdinando Lanza** (1788–1865) had commanded a division under Charles Oudinot during the siege of Rome in 1849. During that campaign his troops were overwhelmed by the ferocity of the bayonet charges led by Garibaldi in the Pamphili Gardens on 30 April and at Palestrina four days later. Obese and unable to ride by 1860, he was 72 years old when he replaced the incompetent Paolo Rufo, Prince of Castelcicala, as governor of Sicily. He had previously served in his native island in 1849 as chief of staff to General Carlo Filangieri, and was best remembered by the citizens of Palermo as a source of amusement for falling into the mud from his horse during a birthday parade for Ferdinand II. Returning to Sicily on 16 May 1860 as an inept field commander, he totally underestimated the determination of Garibaldi and 'the Thousand' during his defence of Palermo. Failing to strengthen his defences at the Porta Termini on 26 May, he slept soundly as couriers pleaded for reinforcement. His decision to order the shelling of Palermo forced the civilian population to completely abandon any semblance of loyalty to the Bourbon Crown and Army.

Frequently described as one of the few charismatic military figures of the Kingdom of Two Sicilies, **Ferdinand Benevento Del Bosco** (1813–81) was born in Palermo and entered the court of King Ferdinand I as a page in 1821. Graduating from the Nunziatella (National Military Academy) in Naples in 1833, he was commissioned as a second lieutenant in the 2nd Grenadiers of the Royal Guard. Often involved in disputes with those in authority, he was dismissed from the Army in 1845 after seriously wounding the militant Bishop Francesco Vassallo in a duel. Granted a king's pardon three years later, he was reinstated with the rank of captain, being awarded the Illustrious Royal Order of St Ferdinand and Merit for bravery while campaigning against revolutionaries in Calabria. Promoted to colonel by 1860, he was ordered to Sicily where troops under his command fiercely defended the approaches to Milazzo. Following the Neapolitan capitulation of that island, he returned to Naples where he was promoted to the rank of brigadier-general on 17 August 1860. Seeking refuge in Naples after the Neapolitan defeat at the Volturno, he was captured and placed on parole, promising not to fight against Garibaldi for two months. His arrival at the fortress of Gaeta in November 1860 lifted the morale of the defenders, although the sally he organized on the 29th of that month failed to break the siege. In Rome by the beginning of 1861, he was expelled by Pope Pius IX for once again being involved in a duel, following which he dwelt in Spain and Morocco, before eventually returning to Naples, where he ended his days.

Another veteran of the Napoleonic Wars, and one of the more reliable Neapolitan commanders, **Giosuè Ritucci** (1794–1869) volunteered for service in the Bourbon Army in 1807. He received the rank of lieutenant in the 2nd Regiment of Light Infantry on 4 November 1811 and in March 1813 was created a Knight of the Two Sicilies, being transferred to the Grenadiers of the same regiment. Promoted to captain on 22 September 1826, troops under his command successfully destroyed a band of brigands operating around Palermo, Trapani, Caltanissetta and Girgenti, in Sicily. He was decorated a Knight of the Order of Francis I on 28 October 1836. A major in the 2nd Chasseurs by 1848, he was wounded in the leg during the rising in Palermo that year, following which he received promotion to lieutenant-colonel. On 15 June 1849 he took command of the 7th Infantry, and by 1853 led the Brigade of Foot Gendarmes. On 19 April 1860 he was promoted to the rank of field marshal, and, following the fall of Naples on 7 September of that year, he was tasked with holding the Neapolitan line north of the river Volturno. Acting on the orders of the King's ministers at Gaeta, he reluctantly divided his force during the ensuing battle, which enabled Garibaldi's smaller army to overcome it piecemeal. Following this defeat, he was appointed governor of the fortress at Gaeta during the siege conducted by the Piedmontese Army, which lasted until the final surrender of Francis II on 13 February 1861.

INSIDE THE MIND

A principal feature of Garibaldi's approach to command in battle was the degree to which he exposed himself to enemy fire. Indeed, he regarded courageous example as the most important rule of engagement, particularly when leading volunteer troops, and on numerous occasions he led from the front. At San Antonio in Uruguay during 1846 he saved the lives of numerous legionaries by leading a night-time bayonet charge, which broke through enemy lines and enabled them to link up with reinforcements. Although wounded, he rallied the Bersaglieri in the Pamphili Gardens and sent French regular infantry reeling back during the siege of Rome in 1849. During the fighting in Sicily in 1860 he again tipped the scales of battle, which possibly marked a turning point in the whole campaign, by leading the final surge that broke the ranks of Sforza's Neapolitan light infantry on the Piante di Romano near Calatafimi. Following his inspirational 'Victory along all the Line' message at the Volturno, his order to fix bayonets and advance proved to be the decisive moment of the battle and, indeed, of the entire Calabrian campaign.

Such leadership was not always beneficial in a tactical sense and Garibaldi admitted being prone to losing sight of the overall course of battle. Of the action at Cerro in Uruguay on 17 November 1846, when he urged his Legion forward with cold steel, he recalled in his memoirs: 'I had allowed myself to be carried away in the charge, like a mere soldier, consequently I only saw what passed around me.' The fact that his enemy often lacked reliable command and leadership, particularly in Sicily in 1860, enabled such reckless conduct to succeed.

When directing troops in battle, Garibaldi was inclined to stand exposed to fire and quietly offer words of encouragement to the young volunteers, many of whom were under fire for the first time. According to Trevelyan, at Milazzo

> the General's exercise of his strange powers of fascination considerably increased the chances of victory. As one section of Dunne's Sicilians with their English officers and cadets filed by him into action up the ride of a cane-brake, he kept repeating in a low voice, 'Avanti! Coraggio, nomini!' When the veteran company of Genoese Carabineers, destined to lose nearly half their number before nightfall, were brought up about ten in the morning to the place where they were to enter the battle, they found the General there before them, standing almost alone in the middle of the road, a conspicuous mark at which the enemy were directing their fire.

The personal bravery of Garibaldi inspired not only his men but fellow officers. The Hungarian Lajos Tüköry was prepared to die attempting to pull down the barricade with his bare hands at the Porta Termini at Palermo, while Nino Bixio continued fighting

Garibaldi wears a version of the red shirt he made famous during various campaigns in this carte-de-visite produced in Naples in 1861. (Author's collection)

In this fanciful Italian lithograph by Cordey, Garibaldi is shown with Vittorio Emmanuele II mounted in the background. (Anne S. K. Brown Military Collection, Brown University)

after cutting a bullet out of his own chest during the same action. The international fame of Garibaldi was such that experienced volunteers from all quarters were prepared to join him in fighting for his cause. From Britain came John Whitehead Peard, John Dunne and Irish artillerist Dick Dowling, while from the United States came ex-filibusters Chatham Roberdeau Wheat and Charles Carroll Hicks, both of whom would soon return home to fight for the Confederate States of America.

The personal magnetism of Garibaldi, and the patriarchal impact he had on the men he commanded, stemmed from early influences. In 1833 he became fascinated by the socialist creed of the Saint-Simonians. Having made a voyage to Constantinople with a group of the apostles of the gospel of the Comte de Saint-Simon as a passenger during his early years in the mercantile trade, he became fascinated by their belief that the man who offered his 'sword and his blood to every people struggling against tyranny, is more than a soldier: he is a hero'. Furthermore, their long red gowns, loose white tunics and black scarves, combined with long hair and flowing beards, remained as a major influence on his flamboyant and patriarchal appearance for the rest of his life.

Although an active Freemason from 1844, Garibaldi had little use for the rituals associated with that organization, regarding it more as a network to unite progressive-thinking men as brothers both within nations and as members of a global community. On the eve of the Masonic Constituent Assembly in Naples in May 1867, he made a famous appeal to all fellow Masons of the Italian peninsula: 'As we do not yet have a country because we do not have Rome, so we do not have a masonry because it is divided… I am of the opinion that Masonic unity will lead to the political unity of Italy.' He was subsequently elected Honorary Grand Master of the Grand Orient of Italy and, following the unification of Italy in 1870, continued to use the ideological cohesion of the Freemasons to promote his plan for the spread of equality and democracy. The extent to which Freemasonry may have helped with the success of his military campaign in Sicily and Calabria in 1860 is not known, although it is entirely possible that links with membership of British, American and even Neapolitan lodges aided his cause, particularly among the ranks of the latter, who were notoriously unreliable as military commanders.

Garibaldi was indeed a complex and controversial character. As an ardent nationalist, he advocated European unity, particularly during the 1870s. As a republican, he served a king and was prepared to hand over his conquest of the Kingdom of the Two Sicilies in 1860 to Vittorio Emmanuele II. Increasingly opposed to the temporal power of the papacy after 1849, and later declaring himself to be 'the avowed enemy of the Papal Anti-Christ', he subscribed throughout much of his life to the anti-clericalism common among many Latin liberals. In 1882 he wrote 'Man created God, not God created Man', yet earlier he had insisted that 'Christ came into the world to deliver humanity from slavery … you have the duty to educate the people … educate them to be Christians – educate them to be Italians… Viva Italia! Viva Christianity!' As a Freemason and pacifist, he spent much of his life as a soldier fighting for a cause. As an international hero who was often compared with Odysseus or Aeneas of Greek mythology, he refused to accept reward and spent his last few years as a farmer.

A LIFE IN WORDS

Well aware of the popularity surrounding his campaigns in South America and Europe, Garibaldi had written his first memoir by 1859. Translated by friend and admirer Theodore Dwight, whom he met during his sojourn in New York City, it was published in New York in 1861 as the first part of *The life of General Garibaldi, translated from his private papers, with the history of his splendid exploits in Rome, Lombardy, Sicily and Naples, to the present time.* The remainder of this volume consists of a narrative produced by Dwight, which is heavily reliant on primary source documents published verbatim. Edited by Alexandre Dumas, who took an active part in the Sicilian campaign in 1860, the memoirs of Garibaldi extending to 1860 were translated into English by William Robson and published in London in 1861 as *Garibaldi: an Autobiography.* Among similar titles, an improved version of this work was published in 1931 with a translation by Robert S. Garnett.

This portrait of an elderly Garibaldi was published in the *Illustrated London News* several weeks after his death in 1882. (Anne S. K. Brown Military Collection)

Garibaldi also wrote three novels, each of which dealt with the experiences of fictional characters set against the background of the struggle for Italian unification. Published in 1870, *Clelia: il governo del monaco* (*Clelia: The Government of Monaco*) was concerned with the persecution of a group of patriots by the Roman government in the period immediately preceding the battle of Mentana in 1867. Also published in 1870, *Cantoni il volontario* was set in 1848–49 and relates the adventures of two members of his beloved Italian Legion during the defence of Rome. Not published until 1874, *I Mille* was about the Sicilian expedition and contained rather more historical fact than the previous two novels.

Of interest, if not entirely reliable, is *Vita di Giuseppe Garibaldi* (*Life of Giuseppe Garibaldi*), which was published in 1882 and produced by writer and philanthropist Jesse White Mario. Born in Hampshire and a naturalized Italian, she served as a nurse with Garibaldi's soldiers from 1860 to 1871. Also serving as a volunteer under Garibaldi in the wars from 1859 to 1871, Giuseppe Guerzoni wrote a two-volume biography of Garibaldi entitled *Garibaldi*, which was published in Florence in 1882.

The redoubtable British historian George Macaulay Trevelyan wrote three thoroughly pro-Garibaldian accounts of the European campaigns. Published in 1907, *Garibaldi's Defence of the Roman Republic* contains an excellent sketch of the commander's early career. It also describes the events leading up to the proclamation of the Roman Republic and provides a detailed and authoritative account of the defence of Rome and of Garibaldi's flight, with a very full bibliography. Turning his attention to the 1860 campaign, *Garibaldi and the Thousand* was completed two years later, followed by *Garibaldi and the Making of Italy* in 1911.

More recent and objective scholarship includes Denis Mack Smith's *Garibaldi: A Great Life in Brief* published in 1956. One of the most important authorities on Italian history, Mack Smith followed this in 1969 with *Garibaldi* as part of a 'Great Lives Observed' series, which includes excerpts from Garibaldi's writings, views by his contemporaries and modern critical assessment. In 1965 Christopher Hibbert produced two comprehensive accounts of the commander, his campaigns and his enemies, entitled *Garibaldi: Hero of Italian Unification* and *Garibaldi and His Enemies: The Clash of Arms and Personalities in the Making of Italy*. While providing a solid look at Garibaldi's life and works, *Garibaldi: Invention of a Hero,* published in 2007 and written by Professor Lucy Riall, of Birkbeck College, is more concerned with the legend surrounding Garibaldi than his achievement on the battlefield. Translated and edited by Stephen Parkin, *My Life*, the new edition of Garibaldi's memoirs in the Hesperus Classics series, is important as it is the first translation into English from his original corrected manuscript, all previous translations having been made from published versions, and often from the original French edition by Dumas.

Recent Italian work has produced *Garibaldi: Citizen of the World* by Professor Alfonso Scirocco, of the University Frederick II in Naples, nearly half of which deals with the life and adventures of the commander before his involvement in the defence of the Republic of Rome in 1848–49 turned him into a popular hero in Europe and North America. Providing an often blow-by-blow account of his many campaigns and battles, Scirocco also examines the evolution of Garibaldi's ideas on war, peace, democracy and society.

BIBLIOGRAPHY

Bampton, Charles (ed.), *Frank Leward Memorials*, London: Kegan Paul, Trench, & Co., 1884

Blackett, Howard, *Life of Giuseppe Garibaldi*, London: Walter Scott, 1888

Brooks, Richard, *Solferino 1859: The battle for Italy's Freedom*, Botley, Oxford: Osprey Publishing, 2009

Casali, Luigi, *Red Shirts: Garibaldi's Campaign in Southern Italy, 1860*, Champaign, Illinois: Ulster Imports, 1989

——, *The Second Italian War of Independence 1859*, Campaign Booklet No. 8, Frei Korps, n.d.

De Polnay, Peter, *Garibaldi, the man and the legend*, New York: T. Nelson, 1961

Dumas, Alexandre (ed.), *Garibaldi: an Autobiography*, London, England: Routledge, 1860

Dwight, Theodore, *The Life of General Garibaldi*, New York: Derry and Jackson, 1861

Evans, Dennis, 'The Battle of Calatafimi, 15th May 1860' in *Miniature Wargames*, No. 40 (September 1986), pp. 32–35

Field, Ron, 'Fighting with Garibaldi' in *Military Illustrated: Past & Present*, No. 131, April 1999

Franzosi, Pier Giorgio, *La Repubblica Romana e il Suo Esercito*, Rome, Italy: Rivista Militare, 1987

Garibaldi, Giuseppe (A. Werner, translator), *Autobiography of Giuseppe Garibaldi*, three volumes, New York: Howard Fertig, 1971

——, (Parkin, Stephen, translator and editor), *My Life (Hesperus Classics)*, London, England: Hesperus Press, 2004

Garnett, Robert Singleton, *The Memoirs of Garibaldi*, New York: D. Appleton and Company, 1931

Guerzoni, Giuseppe, *Garibaldi*, two volumes, Florence, Italy: G. Barbera, 1882

Henty, G. S, *Out With Garibaldi: A Story of the Liberation of Italy*, London, England: Blackie and Son, 1901

Hibbert, Christopher, *Garibaldi and his Enemies: The Clash of Arms and Personalities in the Making of Italy*, London, England: Penguin Group, 1965

Mack Smith, Denis, *Garibaldi: A Great Life in Brief*, New York: Knopf, 1956

—— (ed.), *Garibaldi (Great Lives Observed)*, Englewood Cliffs, New Jersey: Prentice Hall, 1969

Mario, Alberto, *The Red Shirt*, London, England: Smith, Elder & Co., 1865

Mario, Jesse White, *Vita di Giuseppe Garibaldi*, Milan: Treves, 1882

Riall, Lucy, *Garibaldi: Invention of a Hero*, New Haven: Yale University Press, 2007

Ridley, Jasper. *Garibaldi*, New York: Viking Press, 1976

Scirocco, Alfonso (Allan Cameron, translator), *Garibaldi: Citizen of the World*, Princeton, New Jersey: Princeton University Press, 2007

Trevelyan, George MacCaulay, *Garibaldi's Defence of the Roman Republic*, London, England: Longman, Green, and Co., 1910

——, *Garibaldi and the Thousand*, London, England: Longman, Green, and Co., 1912

——, *Garibaldi and the Making of Italy*, London, England: Longman, Green, and Co., 1914

——, (ed.), 'The War Journals of "Garibaldi's Englishman"' Part I, Alps, 1859, *Cornhill Magazine*, January 1908

——. (ed.), 'The War Journals of "Garibaldi's Englishman"' Part II, Sicily and Naples, 1860, *Cornhill Magazine*, June 1908

Verbeck, Peter, *The Garibaldi Panorama*, New York: Dennis Powers Productions, Inc., for Dr James W. Smith, 2004

Viotti, Andrea, *Garibaldi: The Revolutionary and his Men*, Poole, Dorset: Blandford Press, 1979

Winnington-Ingram, Rear Admiral H. F., *Hearts of Oak*, London, England: W. H. Allen & Co., 1889

Plus various issues of the *Illustrated London News*, *Illustrated Times* (London) and *New York Illustrated News*

INDEX